The Young Pobble's Guide to his Toes

by Gavin Ewart

Hutchinson

London Melbourne Sydney Auckland Johannesburg

Hutchinson & Co. (Publishers) Ltd

An imprint of the Hutchinson Publishing Group

17-21 Conway Street, London W1P 6JD

Hutchinson Publishing Group (Australia) Pty Ltd
16-22 Church Street, Hawthorn, Melbourne, Victoria 3122

Hutchinson Group (NZ) Ltd
32-34 View Road, PO Box 40-086, Glenfield, Auckland 10

Hutchinson Group (SA) (Pty) Ltd
PO Box 337, Bergvlei 2012, South Africa

First published 1985
Second edition 1985

© Gavin Ewart 1985

Set in VIP Bembo by
D.P. Media Limited, Hitchin, Hertfordshire

Printed and bound in Great Britain by
Anchor Brendon Ltd, Tiptree, Essex

British Library Cataloguing in Publication Data
Ewart, Gavin
    The young Pobble's guide to his toes.
    I. Title
    821'.912   PR6055.W3

For Julian

This is my son, mine own Telemachus,
To whom I leave the sceptre and the isle –
— *Tennyson*

The Young Pobble's
Guide to his Toes

Acknowledgements

Some of the poems in this book, have appeared in *Ambit, Encounter, Grand Street* (USA), *London Magazine, Maledicta* (USA), *Oxford Poetry, Poetry Review, Spectator, The American Scholar* (USA), *The Honest Ulsterman, The Listener, The Times, The Times Literary Supplement, The Observer, Winter Hotels* (Kings of Wessex Church of England School journal) and in the anthologies *Light Year '84* (USA), edited by Robert A. Wallace, and *New Poetry 9*, edited by Julian Symons. 'Rugger Song: The Balls of the Beaver' has appeared as a pamphlet produced by R.A. Gekoski for The Sixth Chamber Press. Two poems have been broadcast on the BBC's 'Poetry Now' programme. The limerick version of *The Importance of Being Earnest* was written for an anthology of such pieces edited by Eric O. Parrott – *How to Become Incredibly Well-Read in One Evening*. The extract from George Orwell's essay, 'Boys' Weeklies', is reproduced by permission of the estate of the late Sonia Brownell Orwell and Martin Secker & Warburg Ltd.

The words that seem relevant

for the world, which seems
To lie before us like a land of dreams,
So various, so beautiful, so new,
Hath really neither joy, nor love, nor light,
Nor certitude, nor peace, nor help for pain;
– *Matthew Arnold*

Thus we both should gain our prize:
I to laugh, and you grow wise.
– *Swift*

Poets stop writing . . . or they decline into repetition
and self-parody.
– *Fleur Adcock*

Contents

PART ONE

The Young Pobble's Guide to his Toes

Everything comes, everything goes.
Some day you must say goodbye to your toes –
all bitten off by the beasts of the sea
or fading away by a gradual degree,
vanishing into an elbowless night
all blurred and dim in your elderly sight.
The sun goes down and the eyes give up,
your toes will fade, kerflip, kerflup . . .

The moral shines bright as a mermaid's hair.
Count them and keep them while they're still there!

Lights Out

With each new book the old poet thinks:
Will this be the last?
Biros, pencils, typewriters, pens and inks
whisper to him: Get going! Move!
Get it out fast!

Cram the poems in like a herring glut –
two, three to the page!
Randify your writing, riot and rut,
time's short, get out of that groove
they call old age!

Write it all down, write it fast and loose,
it may be sad stuff –
and you were never a golden egg goose –
but shout it out, coming too soon you've
got silence enough!

Singable

Maimed personalities make the best poets still,
with flaws all over the shop,
opium and alcohol, no one could say of them
they never touched a drop –
and there's a strain of reclusive old ladies too
who hardly go out to tea,
agoraphobes, with a murderous loneliness –
not jolly, like you and me –
all the neurotics, the Muse will quite welcome them,
yes, *and* their queerness and quirks,
what does it matter? It turns out so singable,
it doesn't gum up the works!

Acts of Love

*Emily, in reply to Tabby's remonstrances, declared that, if
he was found again transgressing, she herself, in defiance of
warning and his well-known ferocity of nature, would beat
him so severely that he would never offend again. In the
gathering dusk of an autumn evening, Tabby came, half
triumphantly, half trembling, but in great wrath, to tell
Emily that Keeper was lying on the best bed, in drowsy
voluptuousness. Charlotte saw Emily's whitening face, and
set mouth, but dared not speak to interfere; no one dared
when Emily's eyes glowed in that manner out of the
paleness of her face, and when her lips were so compressed
into stone. She went up-stairs, and Tabby and Charlotte
stood in the gloomy passage below, full of the dark shadows
of coming night. Down-stairs came Emily, dragging after
her the unwilling Keeper, his hind legs set in a heavy
attitude of resistance, held by the 'scuft of his neck', but
growling low and savagely all the time. The watchers
would fain have spoken, but durst not, for fear of taking off
Emily's attention, and causing her to avert her head for a
moment from the enraged brute. She let him go, planted in*

a dark corner at the bottom of the stairs; no time was there
to fetch stick or rod, for fear of the strangling clutch at her
throat – her bare clenched fist struck against his fierce red
eyes, before he had time to make his spring, and, in the
language of the turf, she 'punished him' till his eyes were
swelled up, and the half-blind stupified beast was led to his
accustomed lair, to have his swelled head fomented and
cared for by the very Emily herself.

– Elizabeth Gaskell, *The Life of Charlotte Bronte*

1 Traditional

What loving punishment the Lord could give,
a dog's life in the Parsonage, dark graves
where, in the typhus black, their Death could live!

Slab-sided judgment on the dismal tombs!
Drear hopeless hymns, a stern-faced God that saves,
the actual shrivelled flesh they rhymed with – wombs.

They were so little, childlike, small and bent,
large noses, crooked mouths – the 'dear remains'
fitted a child's neat coffin, one long Lent

of self-denial all three sisters kept,
killed by consumption and their dreadful drains.
The words alone flashed out where rainstorms wept!

2 Political

They really loved the Duke of Wellington,
they were a nest of tiny troubled Tories –
as colourful as parakeets and lories,

flaming with passion and 'Thy Will Be Done'.
Yet in that free-for-all, that *fritto misto*,
they didn't truly relish an *aristo*.

The cultured, polished people at the Grange,
the 'plaid silk frock', the 'burnished shoes', 'white
                                        trousers',
meant nothing to these cats – they were all mousers

out on the moors and wild, far out of range.
They never were lukewarm, or smooth, like lotion,
what they liked best was fierce untamed emotion.

Charlotte was adamant in saying how
Jane Austen was all right, after a fashion,
but very superficial, short of passion,

not 'spitted on the horns of a mad cow'
(a very telling phrase of Emily's)
but quite at home in high-born femilies,

without 'fresh air', 'blue hill' or 'bonny beck' –
instead the fenced-in flowers, the fine 'neat borders'.
Almost, all three preferred the lower orders.

3 Personal

Bramwell alone, with the greatest regularity,
filled the old Black Bull with Hibernian hilarity,
just the coarser sex with convivial vulgarity –
        they called him Patrick easily
            when drinkers filled the inn!

Bramwell alone, taking opium with civility,
quickly overturned all his painterly ability,
oh, wasn't he the quare one, with his talkative virility –
        they called him Patrick openly
            when drinkers filled the inn!

Bramwell alone, in that gloomy old sorority,
broke out in a male and a masculine minority,
chasing after tail, with a fig for all authority –
        they called him Patrick drunkenly
            when drinkers filled the inn!

Bramwell alone, with a drinking man's proclivity,
shining like a star as an agent of activity,
acted out the dreams they repressed in their
passivity –
they called him Patrick praisingly
when drinkers filled the inn!

Don't Make Me Hate You!

Foxtrot Song with Introduction

Your jealousy and bad temper –
oh, keep them under control!
What they do to my love for you
is to redefine it and undermine it
like a mole!
I know you're not a phoney,
a pseud or a slut –
so please don't make me
say to myself:
I'm very fond of you BUT . . .

Don't make me hate you!
I'm not happy to hate you!
Please just try to act
with a little . . . tact,
a lass can make a lad
feel so very sad!

Don't make me hate you!
I don't want to hate you!
When those things you say
make my heart turn away
or make me get mad
I feel oh, so sad!

I don't want to leave you –
so don't make me go!
Oh, I won't deceive you,
it's only when you're acting like a
so-and-so
that I want to go!

Don't make me hate you!
I just hate to hate you!
It's when you behave
as though I were your slave –
then I do feel bad,
so depressed and sad!

Aros Castle

I first saw Aros Castle when I was ten, in 1926 –
a ruin with a great ruined window like an eye.
My father took me shooting rabbits. I can fix

all that in my mind. There was a man with a ferret,
the rabbits lived under the rocks, quite near the shore.
I shot my first-ever rabbit. I was proud with acquired
                                                    merit.

And on the small headland the Castle sat still,
looking like a picture postcard view from a window.
After that summer I didn't see it again until

I came to Mull in 1937 (I was twenty-one),
I was reading *Present Indicative*, I'd just finished
                                                    Cambridge,
I had no job in prospect, a lot remained to be done,

it was hot and we drove Margery's car round the
                                                    island roads,
Calgary, Gribun and so on, a lovely summer,
and the Castle still sat there like something with loads

of time on its hands. The eye never blinked or
                                        shifted.
It stood there clear. If it vanished, it would come
                                        back –
as soon as the rain stopped or the mist lifted.

When (in 1967?) I saw it again
I had Margo with me, it was Easter,
a huge rabbit popped up and eyed us with disdain

outside the window, at breakfast. The world had
                                        carried
on with its wars and its worries, the Castle
                                        notwithstanding,
and I had been eleven years married.

That eye never closed. It wasn't designed for sleeping.
It seemed (perhaps this is the pathetic fallacy)
as though it had Time or something in its own
                                        safe keeping.

In 1968 we brought the kids before its unchanging
                                        face.
Jane had to dive into Tobermory Bay from a boat
among a lot of jellyfish. It was part of a race.

And this year, 1981, was (so far) the last time.
I once walked to the Castle – its base is smothered in
                                        nettles
and walking round it isn't much of a pastime.

I think it's nearly 500 years old, but I might be
                                        wrong.
Obviously someone once took trouble to destroy it –
it's a long time since, as a castle, it was really on
                                        song!

Man and boy, you might say, I've been there and
                                        seen it,
as tourist and time-traveller. If they holocaust us
(if Reagan and the Russians really mean it)

I bet that crumbling picturesque dump outlasts us!
Meanwhile it's into thoughtfulness, if not depression,
that that non-seeing picture postcard eye creepily casts
                                                    us.

The Good Companions

They stand behind you and whisper:
Fill your glass! and *Fill your plate!*
Now they are nameless, but later you'll know their
                                                    names,
fiends and familiars with eating and drinking games:
Big Belly and Red Nose and Brain Damage.
They'll find you, sure as fate!

Tip-tankards, they jog the elbow:
Let's finish it! Have the other half!
They'll be your companions throughout your later
                                                    life,
the Knights of the Blissful Bottle, the Knavish Knife,
Lord Blood Pressure, Lady Redvein-Cheeknet,
the lewd litre, the loud laugh!

I could do with a drink! they whisper,
Oh, for a knife! Oh, for a fork!
Though they're refined gourmets and eat a lot of
                                                    French
you'll know them by a very piglike kind of stench,
Lady Burper, Bad Breath, Fartwell –
all dying for the popping of a cork!

A Wordsworthian Self-Apostrophe from the Fourth Floor of the Hotel Admiral (Copenhagen)

Relax. Relax. It's 8 o'clock. The gulls patrol the
                                           harbour.
It's a perfect Danish winter morning.
A man is fooling about with a snow-machine,
a brush that whirrs a pathway on the quay.
A little snow-blizzard looks to be blowing,
but you're inside and warm; with loved ones far
                                           away,
Margo, Jane, Julian, the family names –
Victorian sentimentality, but still are loved ones
and absence makes the heart grow fonder,
though some say out of sight is out of mind.
Wordsworthian thoughts! And soppy Richard Jefferies
prosed of the fine physiques of 'dearest Greece'
(*The Story Of My Heart*, your journey book).

Relax. Relax. The gulls float by the window.
So much of life is so repetitive.
Breakfast comes up, five kinds of bread and coffee.
The roll is hundreds-and-thousands in caraway seeds –
I love the little buggers – remember what Churchill
                                           said
when Admirals plonked Traditions of the Service.
The joy of caraway seeds and coffee!
And you reflect that this is a blue city
and Wordsworth wouldn't have liked it.
Apparently, the sex-shows need a hush,
cathedral silence, solemn and complete –
the man cannot maintain his proud erection
in face of ribald cries, or shouts, or laughter.

Relax. Relax. Baby, it's cold outside!
Life below freezing. The Danish word for scissors?
Your nails need cutting. Such minutiae
aren't part of the egotistical sublime –

but they're important to the traveller.
Long poems spread the inspiration thin
like Danish butter on the varied bread.

And in the night a fucking great ship ties up
(to use the language of sailors) – the *Prinsesse*
Margrethe –
perhaps about fifty yards from the hotel window.
It looks huge and reminds you of Newhaven.

'Hills that purify those who walk on them'
I read in Jefferies. You might as well write:
'Ships that purify those who sail in them'.
The snow keeps up. You mean, keeps drifting down.
All prepositions are a wayward race.

Hot news comes in – a Right Wing coup in Spain.
Young Wordsworth wouldn't have liked it, the old
one wouldn't have cared.
It makes *you* feel quite sick. You're back once more
in 1936, and twenty years old. Spain, a Republic.
You can't do much about it (you couldn't then).
Franco didn't end upside down, like Mussolini.

Abortive – comes the news. Long, sighed relief!

Freedom a topless bar where tits are swinging –
the bad régimes are bras to crowd them in.

Your Copenhagen Guide says 'Topples Girls',
with Spanking, Animal, Rubber, Urine, Chains.

Jefferies gets better – on the Victorian vice of work
and how many millions slave to keep alive –
a kind of blue sky socialism. He didn't believe in God
but neither did he credit Evolution.
In ways, a Lawrence before his time –
in 1883 the legs were limbs.

Oh, such limp verse could limp right on for ever –
as Wordsworth in his garden paced up and down
composing,

26

to spout it all out to Dorothy, a kettle on the boil
and she receptive, humble as the teapot,
ready to write it down.

Relax. Yours is a similar domestic brew.
Drift lazy like the gulls. Sex, love and politics
won't stop for you, an engine idling.
Those gulls bring a message too: relax, relax.

23 February–2 March
revised 28 April, 1981

In Another Country

Our bodies have changed
and are no longer the same
as those that had connection
a quarter century ago;

the scar by the nipple
where the cancer was excised,
the blotch where radiation
burned sore the tender skin;

the womb quite removed;
and a grey white streak
badgers your forehead –
though you still sing in tune.

I too am altering;
fatness and falling hair,
grey at the temples;
wartlike excrescences

appear on my back,
on my arms and legs;
grave-marks on hands.
I'm more like an old frog

27

than I ever used to be,
twinged by arthritis,
gout warnings in toes.
I have more in common

with our vintage cat
than with the children.
All this is not amazing
in a life where old poets

retire into envy
and drink themselves to death
among their admirers
in out-of-the-way places.

Ageing is a faintness
like a line in Shakespeare:
old, old, old, old.
Say it over and over.

Prep School Days

The ivy clusters thickly round the old grey stones. The King is on his throne and the pound is worth a pound. Over in Europe the comic foreigners are jabbering and gesticulating, but the grim grey battleships of the British Fleet are steaming up the Channel and at the outposts of the Empire the monocled Englishmen are holding the niggers at bay.

– George Orwell, 'Boys' Weeklies'

Old Boyce was telling us about Lord Curzon,
how he stood 6ft 3in in his socks
and was Viceroy of India.
In winter the visiting mothers had furs on
when Half Term interrupted timetables and clocks –
and the pitches were windier.

But young Mr Curran, in his suede shoes,
with his pullovers and wavy hair,
said we should be grateful for the Soviet Experiment.
He was new. From Oxford. We accepted his views.
It was the Spanish-named French Master who raged
                             like a bear,
causing dismay and merriment.

He was small but very spruce and dapper,
dented desks with pointers, wore double-breasted
                                 waistcoats
and well-tailored suits.
We read Westerman and Henty and Sapper
and went for seaside walks by the rocks and windy
                                 boats.
In our concrete pool we naked-bathed like newts.

On the nude bottoms, beaten for various offences,
everyone pruriently wondered at the purple-red marks
(did the Art Mistress get quite riggish?) –
we knew little of the sins of the senses.
'Hath he *marks* to guide us to him?' A hymn-joke.
                                What larks!
'Please, Sir, Henderson's being piggish!'

I had homesickness and nervous insomnia,
nightmares, afraid-of-the-dark, even infantile
                               croup . . .
but it's the neurotics that get the books written.
In schola privata pereunt omnia . . .
There's probably a Latin tag in all that alphabet soup.
The Matron said I should read a book called *Every*
                           Inch A Briton!

But I was good at games, with timing if not muscle,
masochist tackler, Captain of the Rugger Fifteen, not
                            too pathetic –
the English Master gave me nothing but praise.
There were two Heads in partnership – Wetherall and
                           Russell.

Russell was fatherly and very sympathetic.
I think of him with a backward love, from those prep
school days.

In the Old People's Home (1914)

This is the last anchorage. HMS *Incontinent*
is in trouble and signals of distress
come from HMS *Repetitive* and HMS *Wanderer*.
HMS *Anxiety* is getting steam up.
The harbour is full of signs of activity,
which are all ignored by HMS *Vainglorious*
as she rides at anchor in perpetual majesty.

Across the water, puffing busily,
come the officious tugs *Snapper* and *Orderly*.

Violent Passions

The mouth can be quite nasty in a bite
The lover's pinch can be malicious too
Legs kick, as well as tangle, in a bed

Words can be harsh and not console or rhyme
Fighting is also love's especial food
Hands can enlace with hands or round a neck

The tools that pierce can be unyielding steel
Attractive nails can score, like claws, the face
Fingers can spread on cheeks, harmful and strong

Hair can be pulled in war, that's stroked in peace
The fighting female differs from the male
The spitting cat attacks the barking dog

Boom Christmas

Because the people of Britain know that the end is
                                                    nigh
and the Instruments of Satan are already installed on
                                      our shores,
they go mad for the Good Life, for the glass and the
                                    food and the thigh,
lusting after Consumer Goods like kerb-crawlers after
                                      whores . . .

They know this is their Last Chance, it may not come
                                            round again,
they know the sizzling turkeys may well be the Final
                                                    Birds
and each one knows what's fried may possibly be his
                                                    brain,
as the comforting Christmas carols ascend in their
                                      fifths and thirds . . .

And all this is traditional, in times of great Dying and
                                                    Plague,
like the Fornication on Tombstones and the
                              Drunkenness in the Streets,
it's a clear indication of a Giant Despair, it's not in
                                      any way vague –
now it means bodies in plastic bags, as once it meant
                                      winding sheets.

The Winter Hotels

Oh, think of hotels where the stars of the bars
          say 'What'll you have?'
and the barmaid's a ringer for an opera singer
          in *Pag.* or in *Cav.*!
They're sad out of season, with very good reason,
          commercials alone

keep the whole thing going, the whisky flowing.
    They lower the tone –
but that bosomy beauty must do her duty
in season and out,
like a loyal Boy Scout . . .

When the men get flirty and jokes are dirty
    as children's knees
(though the family fun is over and done
    and the winter seas
bash the pier about, no one ventures out,
    and the winds are gales)
that's the time when Rosy can feel quite cosy
    with her ring of males,
from richest to poorest (not one is a tourist),
a hub of desire
like a glowing gas-fire . . .

For the mums and dads and the likely lads
    are away and gone –
how could they stay? And that holiday
    has now moved on,
it's there perhaps in the album snaps,
    as the seaweed dries
(that they took from here as a souvenir)
    and the summer flies
that annoyed the drinkers, the laughing winkers,
have buzzed and are dead
by the windowpane's lead . . .

Nobody talks about undercliff walks
    and the lounge's gloom
is deep and dreary, where boozed and beery
    in that roistering room,
with their sexy singing, the boys were bringing
    the place to life –
a tolerant smile, at least for a while,
    on the lips of a wife,
condoned the offence and the pounds and pence,
as the money was spent,
flickered and went . . .

The short winter's day brings blight and decay,
      a pub's like a church
where the evening dims without any hymns –
      and the salesmen lurch
into sweet liqueurs and the brash 'What's yours?'
      like a loud response
echoes in night and the ailing light
      makes bar-sinks fonts.
Though there's nothing wrong with this evensong,
what's worshipped here
is just brass and beer . . .

Gods and Heroes

*And then, like doves or long-winged thrushes caught in a
net across the thicket where they come to roost, and meeting
death where they had only looked for sleep, the women held
their heads out in a row, and a noose was cast round each
one's neck to dispatch them in the most miserable way. For
a little while their feet kicked out, but not for very long.*

    *Next Melanthius was dragged out across the court and
through the gate. There with a sharp knife they sliced his nose
and ears off; they ripped away his privy parts as raw meat for
the dogs, and in their fury they lopped off his hands and feet.*

  – Homer, *The Odyssey* (translation by E.V. Rieu)

Odysseus himself didn't do this – but he ordered it.
He didn't mind being covered in blood and shit.
Victorian Hellenists showered him with love,
equally with Gentle Jesus and the Holy Dove,
they taught the young gentlemen to adore the Greeks
in long school terms that lasted weeks and weeks.
Perhaps as English animal-lovers they found
sentimental satisfaction when the old hound
recognizes him – Odysseus drops a tear –
at his homecoming after the umpteenth year
of fairy story adventures and active fun
(Pallas Athene kept putting blanks in the gun

33

so that *he* always survived, *he* wasn't shot;
his comrades were expendable – Odysseus not.
Not Wanted On Voyage, one could almost say,
as they met sticky ends in every possible way).
Perhaps, too, Victorian eyes grew dim
when his Old Nanny recognizes him.
This also, for her, is a tearful scene.
Though Odysseus, naturally, isn't so keen
to have it known universally that he's back.
He seizes her by the throat and says 'One more crack
out of you and I'll see you meet your death
on the day that all the Suitors run out of breath!'

Odysseus is quite like Hitler – or like Goebbels –
he comes through cruel and sly as Homer burbles
on and on in his primitive masterpiece,
laying the foundation of The Glory That Was Greece;
he couldn't really be much trickier or slyer –
you could call him The Trickster, or even The Liar.

The modern counterpart to fix on
might be, conceivably, Richard Nixon.
Cooling, the earth and planets move –
our politics don't much improve.
We grumble about rates and taxes,
what falls in Africa is axes,
chopping up unwise opponents
into their separate components.

We're civic bees (a liberal hive),
while they skin Russians (and alive)
in not-so-far Afghanistan –
Stalin was much like Genghis Khan
(more devious though) in some respects.
No need to strain your intellects
to see that we've not grown much better
since someone carved that first stone letter.
The ghastly blinkered mad religions
kill unbelievers like rock pigeons.
All Faith, they say, is like a jewel –
but why is it so bloody cruel?

The Bob Hope Classic Show (ITV) and 'Shelley Among The Ruins', Lecture by Professor Timothy Webb – both Saturday evening, 26.9.81

1   Here's the Bob Hope Classic Show,
    devoted to the status quo!
    All the seasoned showbiz comics
    love their leaders, their Atomics
    lost in pools where chicks plunge in
    and the wide-brimmed Texas grin
    isn't black or dispossessed,
    likes big money, girls undressed,
    rides hell for leather, clippity-cloppity,
    at anything that smells of property.

    Money is the Cleopatra
    that seduces Frank Sinatra –
    fat and ugly women too,
    all Republicans, all who
    (lookalikes of old Liz Taylor)
    never dug mad Norman Mailer.
    They have money, and the gumption,
    with conspicuous consumption
    to flaunt how wonderful they are –
    that note they hit will always jar
    while poverty is still around
    and every day is gaining ground.
    A country shared out by the Mafia!
    To call it great – what could be daffier!

    They tie one on, they go on benders, on
    us falls the blight of Dickie Henderson!

2   Eng. Lit. goes hand in hand with Architecture,
        with a small audience, quiet in Keats House
        on that same evening, at a lantern lecture –

the contrast of the mountain and the mouse
you well might think, the caring and the callous,
    the brash unthinking and the ones with nous.

A slide of Shelley (the Baths called Caracalla's),
    he sits there reading with an open collar –
nothing could be more different from Dallas

    and thought that's ruled by the Almighty Dollar –
he liked composing in the free fresh air.
    In that bright landscape he's the bright corolla,

a troubleshooter, like oil's Red Adair,
a man who thought Society should be fair.

Professor Webb tells us that ruins, for *him*,
    weren't simply beautiful or picturesque
(such thoughts were decadent, effete and dim)

    but like a lesson taught from History's desk
that showed how in the end the bad régimes
    were just traced patterns like an arabesque

figuring the desert, scarcely remembered dreams,
    and tyrants ended strictly for the birds
who lived for grandeur and the victim's screams,

    like Ozymandias. The wealth, the herds
of stricken slaves, all vanished in thin air,
    gone like the breath of long-since-spoken words:

Look on my works, ye Mighty, and despair!
Yes, Shelley thought Society should be fair.

And so from ruins what *he* drew was hope –
    unjust societies could lie down and die –
they made his heart leap like an antelope,

he thought that one day there might well be pie
in equal portions shared to one and all
    and not reserved (and doubtful) in the sky.

His optimism, we think, wasn't small.
    Ruins didn't make him sad, quite the reverse,
failure was shadow from a hope so tall

    it spread its radiance into all his verse;
although injustice got into his hair,
    he thought the better would succeed the worse

and never gave in limply to despair –
a man who thought Society should be fair.

Cruel and Unusual Punishments

How a masochist must long for the electric chair!
The wonderful bondage of his/her hands and feet,
the claustrophobic hood fitting over the face,
the metal cap so snug on the shaven cranium,
the plate on the shin and best of all
o best of all
the gagging effect of the mouthpiece –
so leather and lovely
that Spinkelink, asked for his last statement,
could only say 'I can't speak!'
which the Governor elected to take for his last
                                        statement.

Surely one could find volunteers to be electrocuted!
Just as people who agitate to bring back hanging
are always writing in for the job of hangman
or, it may even be, of hangwoman;
they are the sadists, the positives to that negative.

Towards the End of a Novel of 1910: A Passionate Outburst

For nearly a full year
these were the words I dearly longed to hear!
I love you – when you said them in the conservatory,
with the clashing billiard balls just audible
and later the doomful and ominous gong
as it were spreading the news, for from that little
                                                        statement
grows a great volume of sound,
church choirs, responses, vows, vows and vows!

I waited so very long
for those few stuttering notes to burst into song!
I love you – from the prominent bosom and the
                                        narrow-waisted gown
that constricted your softness, I accepted it,
the sigh from your head on my shoulder,
like a waft of cigar scent on some dark summer
                                                        terrace
it flavoured the warmth of the night,
giving rise to events, a smoke message,
                                        important . . .

I had faith and belief,
like a beleaguered town that daily expects relief!
I love you – I knew I should hear it from the
                                        finger-traced lips
and I revolved it in my mind like the
dark brown brandy in the glass,
a pleasure to come, a delight to be savoured,
a future enclosed in a phrase,
so we could go forward like trains at signals greening!

In Memoriam Sir John Betjeman (1906–84)

So the last date slides into the bracket
that will appear in all future anthologies –
and in quiet Cornwall and in London's ghastly racket
we are now Betjemanless.
Your verse was very fetching
and, as Byron might have written,
there are many poetic personalities around
that would fetch a man less!

Some of your admirers were verging on the stupid,
you were envied by poets (more highbrow, more
                                    inventive?);
at twenty you had the bow-shaped lips of a Cupid
(a scuffle with Auden too).
But long before your Oxford
and the visiting of churches
you went topographical – on the Underground
(Metroland and Morden too)!

The Dragon School – but Marlborough a real dragon,
with real bullying, followed the bear of childhood,
a kind of gentlemanly cross to crucify a fag on.
We don't repent at leisure,
you were good, and very British.
Serious, considered 'funny',
in your best poems, strong but sad, we found
a most terrific pleasure.

Christmas Holidays

The Imperial War Museum was once quite small,
housed in part of a building in Whitehall.
I went there in the Christmas Holidays when I was
                                 ten –
standards, pistols, carbines; red squares, charging men
in that partly romantic art that cannot be said to lie
but still doesn't adequately express how woefully men
                                 die.
Uniforms worn by Troopers and Generals, no doubt,
models of guns perhaps – but one thing stood out.

'The skull of a man shot from a gun,' it said.
And there was this unremarkable bony head.

It didn't say who he was, or what he had done.
I realized this was a punishment and not horeseplay or
                                 fun.
I didn't even know for certain if he was killed.
I'd seen a man shot from a gun, and I'd been thrilled.
He landed in a net the other side of the arena,
stood up and took a bow – with a pleased and
                            untroubled demeanour.
Bertram Mills' Circus, a holiday treat, at Olympia.
But here the evidence that he came through was very
                           much skimpier –
nonexistent in fact. I imagined him pushed down the
                               barrel,
then flying through the air like a Christmas carol.
Would he land on his feet, would he be all right?
I pondered these things quite a lot of the night.

I hoped he survived. But the skull? That was a puzzle.
There's a sadistic drawing of a man tied to a gun's
                            muzzle
in Gilbert's *Bab Ballads*; his eyes pop out of his head,
the gunner holds the fire. It's clear he'll soon be dead,
exploded over everything. The best execution to choose
(thought the British in India) because it upset Hindus.

I found out all this, bit by bit, and the more I was
                                        enlightened
the more I became aware of evil, and frightened.
Guilt, Sin, Retribution: tracks in the brain,
                                        deep-grooved.

When I next went there, that exhibit had been
                                        removed.

NOTE *I have been told that the collection I saw was not in
fact part of the Imperial War Museum, but of a similar
institution.*

In Favour of the Greek

Like old men who long for their cocks to
leap up and run like an agoraphobe in the
marketplace to that desirable denseness,

that female festivity where all the
most holy odours dwell, so pleasing to
men and gods, and Zeus in particular,

where the rites are the rites of Aphrodite and
every couch or bed is blessed like a
temple by the glorifying goddess –

like these, at the end of our life, at the
end of a long run in the sand, or a
wrestling or the throwing of a javelin,

we know the Games move to a close for
the other sands run in the hourglasses, also
time is proclaimed by the wet clepsydra

as well as the clepsammia; these are the
stolen hours the poets often take into
their melodious and mythomanic cognizance,

41

and the Games too are only a figure and
our dying eyes can just see the wood nymphs that
are gathering round in a forest of metaphors.

The Black Mass

(See A.E.W. Mason, *The Prisoner in the Opal*)

Who are these people in the room to watch us? They
                              are the initiates –
the ones in cloaks, the ones in masks, the ones
                              shrouded,
the woman of pleasure, the criminal woman, the
                              seeker black with ingratitude,
the bogus intellectual, the Judge with ambitions, the
                              fat aristocrat,
they are in love with malice and wishing for evil.

She is nude as a chicken neck, she lies crosswise,
arms stretched, feet together, she is the altar, a living
                              woman.
The worshippers are muttering and whispering with
                              the hum of bees,
there are wraps, white shoulders, she lies on a black
                              coffin-pall,
her eyes are closed, her breasts rise and fall with
                              tumultuous breathing.

A great lamp in the ceiling throws down light, golden
                              and dazzling.
The celebrant prostrates himself. From silence he
                              begins the service
with the true Mass, the Mass meant to deceive, the
                              Latin prayers,
spoken to entice the True God into the bread and
                              wine,
so that the mockery and the wickedness can begin.

I am wearing the black velvet tunic, the incense hurts
                                                    my eyes,
the scarlet velvet cassock, the lace-edged surplice, the
                                        mask with purple lips,
crowned with the red hair, the Judas colour.
I am a woman like her. In the church I've studied
the wayward swaying of the acolyte.

Nobody recognizes me. Although I'm afraid of him
he's self-absorbed, he licks his lips in triumph,
he hardly notices me. I know the occult backwards,
I worked in a library once from M to O,
I know how Christ hangs upside down on his cross.

They are all masked except him. She wears a black
                                                silk mask,
she too is deep in an aura of triumph, her eyes shine
                                                    bright,
he has the priest's cassock, the alb and stole. He is
                                                dreaming,
as I swing the gold censer by its linked gold chains,
remembering history's brilliant followers of Lucifer.

The light falls downwards on the cold clear picture –
she crosses herself upwards, not downwards, with her
                                                    thumb –
she only is important and Adonis is important,
there will be a sty of animals met in a battle of lust,
but still the fine young god dispenses only the cold.

I look beyond my long-curled-delicate-eyelashed mask
and see the picture. Adonis the Sterile, Satan –
The Grimoire of Honorius advocates murder –
the two big golden six-branched candelabra,
with tall black candles stinking with sulphur and pitch.

On one panel naked figures dancing back to back,
white fat human faces, pain, rewards and tortures
and Satan's blue eyes that burn unbearably bright,
unutterable sadness, a youth, slender, erect,
white as a girl, the face too delicate.

And now the spoiled priest calms the blasphemies
and leads them to his purpose. As at the sacred climax
a great trembling takes her body and limbs, cries
                                        uttered low
like the whimperings of an animal, I see that still
my bracelet haunts her wrist, good evil omen.

He holds the chalice high above his head,
places it down between her breasts, three times.
The third time, and the cries become one long-drawn
                                        wail,
a strong convulsion shakes from head to foot,
her arms relax, a rattle scours her throat.

The knife comes down, the hidden knife comes
                                        down,
the blood runs into the cup, a broken, conjuror's
                                        rhythm,
I am the magician's girl who does not flinch:
'Now, if ever, greet your worshippers!
You have a sacrifice worthy of you! Come, oh come!'

The knife hilt upright, shafted in her flesh.
Above her heart one breast is striped with blood.
I am exhausted, frozen, I know I still must run –
until the cloak is thrown over my head,
the hand over my mouth. I do faint then.

Innocence

*'I love these little people; and it is not a slight thing when
they, who are so fresh from God, love us.'*

– Narrator in *The Old Curiosity Shop* by
Charles Dickens

No, not so.
Babies love only themselves
and think the whole world is there for them.

Children are selfish
and learn only slowly not to grasp and grab.
Even the cutest kid
is far less Ego than Id.

In 1940,
a hundred years after
Dickens went so overboard for Little Nell,
that Adolf Hitler
was plastering England with jealous bombs
in a childish rage
only enemy blood could assuage.

Yet they *have*
an innocence, they're honest,
the one thing they can't do is pretend,
infants speak true,
what they feel they certainly show.
They're not divine –
but they're not hypocritical swine.

Robert Graves

When Robert Graves got involved
with a wildly unsuitable woman
his problems were *not* solved –

though he, later, did get married
to a much more suitable woman.
But he was considerably harried

by an arrogant arid virago –
a madly unsuitable woman.
If he'd sailed off in an Argo

like Jason, and left them all screaming
(each clearly unsuitable woman),
it might have been better – but dreaming

of Goddesses (White) and of Muses
(the *younger* unsuitable woman)
is what the male masochist chooses!

O Governesses and O Nurses!
From the strains of Unsuitable Woman
came the excellence of his verses!

Are You Married or Do You Live in Kenya?

(A Young Man Projects Himself into a High Life Fantasy)

I'm there in the Aberdare Highlands
with Diana and Joss – and all the others –
where all the little drinkipoos
can make us fairly stinkipoos
and you can't identify the fathers,
though you know the mothers
(oh yes, you very definitely know the mothers).

I'm there in the twenties and thirties,
drinking in Tart's Hotel and the Gin Palace,
voyeurs bore holes in bedrooms
and what's done in the said rooms
is known to all the decadent de-lovelies
who admire the Phallus
(it really is White Worship of the Phallus).

So many names with 'de' as prefix!
Lord de Robinson will be *my* handle –
half-seas-over, floating seawards,
Idina blows the feather mewards . . .
it's sixty-nine perhaps, with a new partner,
or putting out the candle
(old dirty talk said 'putting out the candle').

46

Zebras, leopards, herds of eland,
a lovely landscape makes us all light-headed
as much as sexy joys do
(hard work is what the boys do),
wives are in common here and so are husbands,
no woman goes unbedded
(the Old Etonians see they're not unbedded!).

NOTE   *See* White Mischief *by James Fox, concerning the murder of Lord Erroll by a fellow-Etonian.*

Places

Some poets love a county like a person –
and that could certainly be said of Gurney,
who made a Mecca almost out of Gloster,
bright as a star in childhood's Christmas stocking.
Imaginary but real, like thoughts of Heaven,
these local habitations have them bending,
Powys with Glastonbury, Housman's Shropshire,
Hardy with Dorset and his Cornwall doggy,
and Norman Nicholson alone in Millom,
all mixed in admiration, blended figgy
pudding and waits and dancing, Nine Men's Morris
and everything old and sanctified with honour.
The fiddlers play, and all the world goes round.

But I could never think like that of London,
London is good and bad, a teasing monkey
(remembered from a kids' book with a moral),
and not for worship in such all-out postures.
You know it, you can't love it, it's all changing,
it's not like Wenlock Edge or any fable,
the fine white buildings are its best of beauty,
it isn't sweet or quaint or bathed in cuteness,
it isn't Rome, New York, or French like Paris –
part stately, scruffy, treeful, never ranting
or boastful (though so praised by Dr Johnson),
it's not a dove, a sparrow, or a condor.
The thinkings that *I* feel don't make a sound.

I.M. Anthony Blunt

ob. 26 March 1983
Portsea Hall, Paddington

They took your body, in its coffin, to a battered
                            whitish van,
  quite plain,
from the flat that held the Poussin. Only classic
                            Poussin can,
  unstirred,
  remain
quite so classically unaltered by the fate of mortal
                            man –

  no word
  of pain

ever shakes the dancing shepherds or the clear blue
                            summer sky.
  It's sad
you were shaken by a maverick clever buccaneer like
                            Guy.
  You had,
in one sense, a lot of genuine pressing thirties
                            reason-why.
  Good, bad,

who should say, who saw the Fascists creeping up the
                          'Europe' map?
  Dead? Red?
Both together not unusual! Hitler was the kind of
                            chap,
  some said,
who stopped commies. Race against time! And the
                        last important lap!
  He *led*!

Pressmen, who would sell their mothers for a
                                        front-page story's sake,
    howled loud,
threw your fox-name (it was easy, just a piece of Fleet
                                                Street cake)
    to the vast
    hound-crowd.
I remember charm and knowledge, wit too – *that* was
                                        never fake –
    time past
    allowed.

Parnassian Conversations

I should be very mean indeed
if I ever criticized you for not being 'literary'
or not liking conversations that are Parnassian,

though this is the stuff on which some wives feed
and go for at parties, who make merry
in front of the Pashas and gyrate like Circassian

slave-girls at the Court of a Bard!
I don't want in any way to bend your nature –
after all, I can't sing in tune, I'm not numerate.

People are people, it would be very hard
if there were some piece of Lit. Law or legislature
that said everyone had to have the same sense of
                                        humour! It

would be cruel and useless to say 'Love Hardy, or
                                        else . . .'
not everyone is sensitive to nuances that are verbal,
even God is in the end a matter of personal opinion –

I can't jump on you like policemen with big boots,
                                    ski jumpers at Hels-
inki, for not skipping through Ashbery like a gerbil!
Your love is far more important than Yeats or
                                    Laurence Binyon!

Only a Few Thousand Can Play

Poetry is a very ancient indoor game
like chess and draughts and knucklebones;
it can arouse emotion, it can be fun,
but you must always remember the galaxies
where the writ of T.S. Eliot does not run,

and the streets that are full of don't-knows
with other ways of using spare time;
verse-writing is a hobby, or a craft,
pursued by the uncommitted singleton
who into a great sea launches his raft,

not knowing quite where he will land or how,
if the rough rhymes will hold the logs in place
or the dovetailing stand the tall waves.
It's only then that the artificer
sees how, in rough weather, it behaves.

Can a Woman Be a Shit?

Can a woman be a shit?
The short answer, I'm afraid, is Yes –
though you would never guess
when a lesbian feminist bursts into song,
saying how no woman can ever do wrong, or be
                                            wrong!

It's an insult just for men,
everybody has always said and thought;
they say good manners ought
to stop us using it when ladies are concerned,
but to tell the truth (not just female truth) it's often
                                                    earned.

How could Evil have a sex?
It certainly doesn't have an age,
though on a Victorian page
you will find the innocent purity of the child.
But don't believe it! Evil's a card that's always wild.

Mysterious Africa

Sonnet Parnassien

Our ships around her coasts make daily nibblings
And touch her inlets and her deeper bays;
Mostly they unload and sail in a few days.
She is alone, a country without siblings.

Her dark interior, how sinister or happy?
Larger, at least, than any sailor knows.
We know giraffe, elephant, water buffaloes
(Tales of gorillas, cannibals, okapi) . . .

Zebra, lion, antelope are like small change –
But her exotic miles hold more than these,
Legends that we can misapply and bungle,

Beyond our limited nineteenth-century range,
Pygmies, they say – or giants tall as trees?
She keeps her secrets in her solid jungle.

What's in a Marriage?

Nobody knows what goes on in a marriage.

–Stewart Scott

Outsiders never see the inside –
what happens behind closed doors
they guess from the raised or succulent voices,
the dark cries of 'You bastard!'
or an ecstatic 'Oh, darling!'
(the things that don't get into Poetry Book Society
Choices)

if they ever get so near the inside!
Mostly, at a party, a slip
or a metaphorical hem is showing,
there's a mood hinted at,
a two-way exchange of feeling,
an atmosphere of Before-the-Storm, or After (the
thunder going).

There are lots of bullies on the inside,
weeping blackmails fill a room,
and quarrels stem from slight, or from very lost,
causes.
Outsiders don't hear that
hidden passionate music –
they see the violins and trumpets poised only, during
pauses . . .

Deathbeds

In the old days when people died
the whole family gathered round the bed
standing or kneeling (patriarchal or matriarchal)
and the last frail blessings and goodbyes were
said . . .

and people also said things like 'His race is nearly run'
and 'Fear no more the heat o' the sun',

and the old cock had fallen into desuetude
and the womb no longer wept its blood –
yet the children stood there (filial and familial)
by the upright grandfather clock's sad ticking thud,
and everybody's tears made it an occasion not to be
                                                    missed
as the last dutiful kisses were kissed . . .

but now they are spirited away, behind curtains,
hidden in hospitals, wrapped warm in drugs,
they don't see the kids for whom (paternal or
                                            maternal)
they had the love; and solitary, slower than slugs,
the unconscious hours move past them. Nobody
                                        wants to know
or cares exactly when they go . . .

The Man in the Opera Sings to His Loved One

You're like the jolliest picnic in a children's book,
like the bright sun in the morning is the way you
                                                look,
you're just the most beautiful dish that any cook
                                            could cook!

I simply adore kissing your ears and your toes,
it's all the course of true love – that's the way it
                                            goes –
you're wonderful enough to cancel out a whole
                                    weekful of woes!

I feel terribly happy that I'm the one you like,
my desires all run away with me like a racing bike,
I am amplified like the song that goes into the mike!

53

And all I can think about is: What did I ever do
to deserve the First Prize of a marvellous person like
                                                    you?
Hooray! that Fate singled me out to be the head of the
                                                  queue!

Some Say

Some say
life is cheerless,
as when the son realizes
that the dead mother
has gone for ever
and all the variously-loved-ones
gone for ever . . .

Some say
there is a Heaven
where we meet again
those we want to meet –
but suppose some others
don't want to meet them
now or ever?

Some say
all you can hope for
is to practise an art,
do well with your work,
love a few people;
failures, successes
don't last for ever . . .

Into History

Marched eighty miles in five days; crossed a river.
We were going to cross, they said, another river – but
the nearest crossing was blocked by their 6000.
For five days, and hungry, we marched the river
                                                    bank,
the enemy keeping pace on the northern side.
On the sixth, a forced march across a plain,
we got ahead; two damaged causeways, hasty
                                                    sappering,
and we were over.

Two hundred miles or more in twelve starved days.

October 20. Scarcely a day's scarce rest.
October 21. Marched eighteen miles;
the next three days, another fifty-three.
Three marches more, they said, and we'd be safe –
the port, and home.

October 24, late in the day, the scouts came back.
Enemy ahead, they said, deploying for battle.

That night round a little village, clustering in,
ate skimpy rations, confessed sins, heard Mass,
and armed for battle.

At first light, knights and archers out.
A thousand yards ahead, across the field,
we saw the enemy, between the eachside woods,
stand or sit idle, breakfasting, with jokes,
some getting fighting-drunk (*our* wine was small!) –
such confidence in numbers, vast superiority.
The archers dug in stakes for cavalry.

Three or four hours of waiting, worst of all.
Cold muddy ploughland, sown with winter wheat.
So short of food nine days, nuts and berries
the archers' feeding. Rainwet and cold,

stood in our ranks, many with diarrhoea
but anchored there, mail leggings laced to plate
                                        armour,
foul with discomfort.

The order to advance. We stumbled slow and cold
over ploughed ridges. And into History . . .

NOTE   *See the account of the battle of Agincourt (1415) in*
The Face of Battle *by John Keegan.*

Father Love

To see you standing there, a great big beautiful son,
twenty-three years old and back from two months in
                                        America,
gave me a pang; it was love, it was seeing a vision,
it was what Margo your mother was obviously
                                feeling, with kisses;
for women, in spite of the Sisters, can have sons and
                                love them.
But men kissing and holding aren't really part of our
                                culture.
It's the slap on the back, something more than a
                                handshake
yet not as emotional as the arms-round embrace.
I stood there. I was happy – but I never touched you.
I was pleased, I was proud as a parent, I said 'Hello,
                                fruitcake!'
or some other greeting, banal from the Marx Brothers
                                thirties . . .

That's the way it takes us, but it wasn't always so.
There were days of no stiff upper lip and no biting
                                back tears.

America, some say, is a big crooked country
and has been since the Volstead Act and Jesus Saves
got it organized for crime (with what good
                                    intentions!) –
but you weren't coming back from the dead or some
                                    Ultima Thule,
although I suppose you could have been shot by a
                                    lunatic.

So perhaps emotion wasn't in place; but, once, men
                                    wept openly
and threw their arms about, hugging the prodigals
and squeezing the loved ones, both breathless and
                                    tearful.
I think the Greeks did, and even the Romans
who thought fairly highly, their books say, of
                                    hardness
and all the republican virtues. They did, yes, I think
                                    they did.

We are so used to the thought that nothing is perfect.
A novelist invents a most attractive girl with a nose
                                    like a ski jump
and we know for certain that (as with the moon)
                                    there's always a dark side.
But this was unlooked for and happy, pure gold on
                                    the stream bed
or a delicious chocolate coming random from the
                                    box.

St Syphilis and All Devils

As I sit eating a Heinz Big Soup
I can hear the choir of St Syphilis and All Devils:
they are singing for me in a little chapel-of-ease,
part of the ruins of St Erysipelas-the-Less.
Big Nasties in their robes conduct the service.

The motorways are chill, and cold the concrete,
there is no nourishment in a spaghetti junction,
the foods and wines are trapped in cold tin
as everywhere the sleety rain comes down .
and all the cars whizz past like lions and demons.

Unemployed boys are freezing in disaster,
the frizzy-haired girls are cold as Eskimos,
everything is packaged, disaster is packaged,
human contacts are the taunts and stabbing,
dead boredom at home, outside the hellpacks . . .

And now they unwrap the little packaged wars
lodged in their tinsel at the foot of the Christmas tree,
there are little bangs and crackers; but the big presents
remain to the last. Who will get what? All the
                                            choristers
rise and explode in a giant crescendo . . .

Rusted iron in broken concrete and thin dead trees.
Clear on all the transistors that demonic choir
is singing enthusiastically of human breakdown,
fat fiends in surplices, St Syphilis and All Devils:
working for a profit, putting *us* in the collection.

'If'

If you can keep your head when all about you
    Are losing theirs and blaming it on you;
If you can trust yourself when all men doubt you,
    But make allowance for their doubting too:
                                    etc., etc.

My mother had it at home, framed on a wall.
Now, much less seriously, it's in the loo
(Kipling's Commandments) but still advice that you,
if you're wise, wouldn't deride at all.

The first two lines seem made for family rows
(it has a sort of floral, mistletoe, border);
'It's asking a lot!' my daughter says. Tall order
most certainly, fuller of whats than hows!

What feminist would want to be 'a man'?
Protestant work-ethic, stern and stoic;
might make a prig – but not a political cat –
yet it's consoling for the also-ran,
though we can mock, more humble than heroic,
we still can see what he was getting at.

Grandfatherism

If they want to make me a grandfather,
my children will have to hurry up –
I'm rapidly approaching that point of no return
where animated bust (or storied urn)
or mute verbosity of paper verse
are all that can go further than the hearse . . .

so, although the heart warms for children
(it's narcissism but universal),
no one may ever say 'Don't wake up Grumpy!
He's very tired!', 'Don't shout, it makes him jumpy!'
and the versatility of the genes
(that adds up to more than a row of beans)

may never be made manifest in my case.
I might be liverish and bad-tempered
and, if so, I apologize, well in advance –
I shall be past my best. And if, by any chance,
the little voices fall on my deafening ears,
they may have come too late – by a matter of twenty
                                              years.

Conversation with a Friend in Cambridge

I seriously thought of writing this poem in the style
of Henry Newbolt, in the style of 1906, because at the
moment I have his *Selected Poems* to review, because
he (like my father) went to school at Clifton, because
my father was up at Christ's in 1906; there were
many complicated and sentimental reasons. Also,
more obscurely, because my father was thirty when I
was born and I first met you when I was an
undergraduate at Christ's in 1936 – thirty years after
he was there in 1906. O numerology!

So it's a long time, and forty-one years I should
guess since I saw you last.

So the conversation had to be about who was still
alive (the first consideration), about what they were
doing now. The obvious usual under such
circumstances. But also about that vanished
Cambridge before Petty Cury was a pedestrian
precinct, before the War, even. *Le monde
d'avant-guerre*, as the French might say. As Henry
Newbolt would certainly say: about Youth.

About who was in love with who (a grammarian
would say 'with whom'), who liked, who more than
liked; and in that not completely unchanged
Cambridge summer I tasted again the bitterness and
the sweetness of that time. The hardness of growing
up, the shyness that was painful. You told how
somebody who was thirty (a great age to people of
eighteen) explained to you how the good thing about
growing older was that you became less shy.

But we move on, everybody moves on. Youth has its
joys and its great unhappinesses. Nostalgia, longing to
go back? That's the last journey I would want to
make. No sensible person would ever want to be
young again. If we die in a time of peace we shall lie
cooling in a hospital, the orifices plugged with cotton
wool or wearing a sort of nappy (second childhood
indeed!) before they put us into the freezer to await
cremation or burial. But the people one likes are still
the people one likes . . .

Fair Women

When I was young
I used to see the
photographs in the paper
of the women for whom men
had seen fit to do murder:
big battleaxes or only half-pretty,
hauled into some court in some city.

They didn't seem
at all attractive –
photographs show most women
(at least the snapshotty ones)
not much apt to coax semen;
and in those prison-van circumstances
their charms didn't have the best of chances.

They weren't like stars
that gleamed on screens (like
shining-haired Joan Bennett);
with their supporting police
they were more like Mack Sennet,
bulging old bags, the targets for crowd hisses –
I couldn't imagine covering them with kisses.

But now I know
two people only,
always, are involved there –
and this is more of a mystery
than Holmes ever solved. There
is no place for cameras or other outsiders –
the only third person is Love, with her blazing
                                        outriders.

As each stood,
her V of hair dark,
so clearly, perfectly naked,
she seemed a goddess perhaps,
the man was proud to make it,

that love – the V between her legs a Y and furry,
her face in close-up (as photographed later) blurry . . .

On top of them
the men lay hard, and
sucked their pinksoft nipples
(they might have been terrible hags
or sluts – that view's other people's)
until long hatreds built up, or short quarrels,
to Death – nothing to do with photography or morals.

Three Weeks to Argentina

Shall I wave my little
Union Jack?
Shall I go all out for
a big attack?
Shall I sing: 'My country
right or wrong!'?
Shall I rattle out a
sabre song?

Or shall I write of
sailor boys
deep in the sea, that can
make no noise?
Or of feckless, careless
young marines
missed by the girls
and the wet canteens?

It's hard for an old man,
who's seen wars,
to welcome that devil
and his claws.

They reach from the ocean,
clash in the sky,
make the earth into
a shepherd's pie.

Professionals love it,
the admirals all,
a chance to show that they're
on the ball.
Newsmen like it,
because it's news –
but fathers and mothers
have different views.

17 April 1982

Did You See the Ace of Spades?

*Tilly told me lots of bitchy stories about Adele Astaire . . .
'She saw me with Friedrich and with Prince Obolensky;
she is very jealous of these two tall, handsome men; she is
so hot to get a man and is so unable to. She has quickies
with the stage-hands. She calls them into her dressing-room
and they have her on the floor.'*
   *. . . I became rather cold towards Adele. She was rather
wild. I remember once in New York, she got out of my
Rolls-Royce on my side, by lifting her legs over the gear
lever, and deliberately showing everything in so doing. She
saw the expression on my face and said, 'Oh, hello! Did
you see the ace of spades?'*

– Edward James on Tilly Losch and Adele Astaire,
The Observer, 18 July 1982

Fred and Adele Astaire!
Like Mickey Mouse and Minnie Mouse,
the simple innocent dancers!
Lady, Be Good! was there,
written in lights, the Empire, Leicester Square –

the songs, but not the show
(1928 and I was twelve)
because of the gramophone records
I did indeed know!
They still carry a strong nostalgic glow.

And, later, *Funny Face*,
this one I certainly saw,
puberty's edge, or just after –
but the blood didn't race
in heart, pulse or that forfended place.

She simply seemed quite cute,
comic and with no hint,
as she tap-danced with her brother,
of old forbidden fruit,
diamonds, spades or any other suit . . .

It's nice to know, with age,
that she was human too
(though who trusts feminine gossip?),
sexy, out of the cage,
and lived where lionsize desires rage . . .

After those five decades,
and I'd never seen it then,
(she aristocratically married),
though all desire fades,
I know a lot more about the ace of spades.

The Mischievous Boy

Love jumped on us before we knew his name,
twisted our arms at prep schools,
hid up our mothers' skirts,
oh! we were bent
by knitted bosoms
and that ladylike scent!

64

Love was a tyrant in his belted shorts,
was good at games and comely
just as the Bible said,
behind the scrum
a hardworked angel –
no wicked words like bum.

Love came, not physical in any way;
demanding friendship only,
the simple name of friend
was all we sought –
but his refusal,
what hellish pain *that* brought!

The Town Mouse and the Country Mouse

The country poets – Thomas, Gurney, Clare –
loving the landscapes, treescapes, cloudscapes,
seem far removed (as Hodge from Fred Astaire)
from all the sly sophisticated Byrons
who delight only in a town's environs.
The Mount of Venus is the hill *they* see,
where every hair in close-up is a tree.

For city-dwellers fields are cold and wet –
and full of dimwits, rustics, clodhoppers,
though land means money (no Lord can forget).
In overlordship they were unforgiving
and Clare, we know, could barely scrape a living.
The prosperous farmer never saw much harm
in the forced labour of his prosperous farm.

Patrons and peasants both, they could agree
that land's not landscape, treescape, cloudscape.
Crops from the soil and apples from the tree,
all of it business, warlike, they were waging –
there was a price on what looked so engaging.
Romantic barren land was not much good;
except as timber, who could love a wood?

The Puritans

The generally held view is that it's the ascetics
who think sexual intercourse so appalling,
and what in pop songs used to be called falling
in love; they use words like 'lusting'
and think it's all disgusting.

But in fact it's the homosexuals, male or female,
who really go off course and scream, and shudder
like a ship blown onto the rocks without a rudder,
at the idea of men and women copulating
and the warm wet of mating.

The attitude to the parents, perhaps? or are they
                                        jealous,
knowing they won't succeed in restraining
these heretics in marriage beds who're staining
the sheets with that tribute all must render,
as love's made flesh, and tender.

The Falklands, 1982

This must have been more like the Boer War
than anything seen in our lifetime,
with the troopships and the cheering,
the happy homecoming, the sweetheart-and-wifetime,
everything looking over and solved,
and no civilians involved –

except a few stewardesses, Chinese in the galleys
almost by accident taken
willy-nilly on The Great Adventure,
where the Argentine fusing of the shells was often
                                        mistaken –
lucky for each floating sitting duck.
Oh yes, we had luck!

66

Luck that the slaughtered World War I soldiers
who died on the Somme and at Arras
would have welcomed, in their dismal trenches –
though that's not to belittle the victory of the Paras,
who lost, all in all, very few dead,
good men, well led.

At home, indeed, it was terribly like the World Cup,
though far less bright, commentated, stagey,
security making the war news nil, mostly,
but good value when they finally stopped being
cagey.
Was the *General Belgrano* really offside?
A few hundred died.

And the outstanding achievements of the great Press,
particularly that section called 'yellow',
that wrote 'Up yours!' on missiles, went berserk
and shouted 'GOTCHA!' in a giant coward's bellow –
and circulation rises, like *The Sun*.
But was it well done?

Kipling's 'Recessional' told us to beware of Hubris,
and not give way to flag-waving
(they don't in the Lebanon, or Northern Ireland) –
if men's lives are worth giving, they're also worth
saving.
Who let them start the bloody thing?
That's the question, there's the sting.

PART TWO

The So-Called Sonnets

Sonnet: Pepys in 1660

Everybody is openly drinking the King's health!
The King is about to be back! There are bonefires
                                              everywhere!
Stable government, King and Parliament, not
                                    Cromwell's wobbly son!
Yet Pepys, at sixteen, saw with satisfaction the King's
                                              beheading.
'There's a Divinity doth hedge a King,
rough-hew him how we will!' – Samuel Butler's joke.
Charles II promises a free pardon,
proceedings only against those named by Parliament.

As you read, you can see what is coming.
Exhumation and gibbeting of regicides –
hanging, drawing and quartering for those still living.
We are still in the century when Shakespeare died,
where the racks and the fires were not thought
                                              barbaric . . .
with Pepys, his music, his ideas of order, a civilized
                                              man.

NOTE   *20 October 1660 'I saw the limbs of some of our
new Traytors set upon Aldersgate, which was a sad sight to
see; and a bloody week this and the last have been, there
being ten hanged, drawn, and Quartered.'*

                                    – *Samuel Pepys,* Diary

Sonnet: Equality of the Sexes

I'm sure if I were a woman I should hate
being regarded as someone designed by Nature
to answer the telephone, make sandwiches, make tea;
or be fucked, look after a family, wash, cook, sew.
I would want to be an engineer, I would want to be
                                                    regarded
as a person whose sex, though inescapable, was
                                                    accidental
and not of the first importance. Though we don't
                                                    deny
there *are* maternal feelings – and traces of
                                        masochism . . .

still, though men are in the rat race, and the American
                                                    Satan
with not much help from others could burn us all up,
even so – if men are devils – we mustn't think all
                                                    women
are perfect, downtrodden angels. There are nasty
                                        people about
of both sexes – surely you know some? Equally nasty
(or equally nice?) – that's one 'equality of the sexes'.

Sonnet: Your Turn in the Barrel

There's an old dirty story that goes like this:
There were seven men in an isolated mining
                                        community.
One, lately joined, asks 'What do you do about sex?'
'Well, you see,' they say, 'we have this barrel.
There's a special hole in it, very conveniently placed.
Every day one of us, naked, gets into the barrel. He's
                                        there all day.
Joe on Monday, Ike on Tuesday, Bruce on
                        Wednesday – and so on . . .'
'But what about Sunday?' 'That's your turn in the
                                        barrel.'

Surely this is a very potent parable.
Writers can always bear the criticism of others.
Criticism of *them*? They don't much like it.
Also, it applies to the deaths of other people –
most of us face them with some equanimity.
It's only when it's our turn that we seem much
                                        moved.

Sonnet: Snobs' Corner

When my daughter Jane went to the Holland Park
                                        Comprehensive
she sat with two friends who had been at her Primary
                                        School –
because they were bourgeois (one of them even an
                                        aristocrat)
they all three spoke the BBC's standard Southern
                                        English,
without a trace of the surrounding glottal Cockney.
At once they were mimicked, called toffee-nosed and
                                        snobs.
The slurrers and h-droppers christened them Snobs'
                                        Corner
(and indeed they weren't Cockneys, Irish or West
                                        Indian).

This was all – in a roundabout way – good for them,
to meet unprivileged, poor people on equal terms.
But what I ask is, wouldn't it be better
if instead of the Two Nations, the Posh and Dustbin
                                        education,
free or fee-paying, some effort was made to spread it
                                        all equally?
To get the rulers and the ruled on the same side of the
                                        fence?

Sonnet: Supernatural Beings

You can't ever imagine the Virgin Mary having
vulvitis or thrush –
she's not a real woman, she's a supernatural being,
not like the real women who are snoring and farting.
Aldous Huxley in an essay said that the angels
painted so often in Italian pictures
would need huge pectoral muscles if they were ever
to fly . . .
But angels, like the Virgin, are supernatural beings.
It's all done by magic. If you can, you believe it.

And not so much *if you can*, more *if you want to* –
if you want to imagine something a bit kinder than
people,
full of love and bursting with benevolence
you go for these smiling supernatural do-gooders
that look a little patronizing to an ordinary man
and still can't prevent you getting cancer or a cold.

Sonnet: Going to 'Guys and Dolls'

Of course, as soon as you add music, the whole thing
                                                changes.
Music can make even misery into beauty.
The small-time crooks, the tricksters, murderers, of
                                                the thirties
become somehow charming eccentric characters –
like the eighteenth-century highwaymen in *The
                                                Beggar's Opera*
who can all sing in tune and seem romantic,
or the starving students in the jollity of *La Bohème*.
The music gives everything an extra dimension.

Does it falsify? It's bound to falsify.
All music is always a great cheerer-upper.
Even the rough sound of the populist screaming
is mild compared to the hangovers and bad trips,
the sad teenagers, with unemployment hanging round
                                                their necks.
You can transmute it, through a trumpet or a
                                                saxophone.

Sonnet: Playing for Time

This was the telefilm of women in Auschwitz,
written by Arthur Miller, with Vanessa Redgrave
as the lean head-shaven French nightclub singer
in the camp orchestra – a great performance.
One critic called it Daughter of Holocaust
(a critic must have his little joke)
but it's only right we should be reminded
how racism persists right into the gas ovens (Jews
                                    and Poles)

though humanity, common to all, should bridge the
                                    gap.
And how all these things did actually happen.
From stress and malnutrition they stopped
                                    menstruating,
their shaved heads too made them look sexless –
they could have been men. All you could say was
(and this was perhaps the point) they all looked
                                    human.

Sonnet: The Power of Sex

While you're doing it, the love is genuine.
The animal tenderness wrapped in soft skin!
An impulse of real love, you're filled to bursting,
the caresses are their own love declaration,
however transitory it is, quick or commercial.
No Great Romance could do better,
speeches and attitudes and sensibility
much less Things In Common and Standard
                                        Marriage . . .

But if you look in the eyes of a dog that's fucking,
he has an unaware, abstracted look.
He looks as though he isn't enjoying it much,
a question of physical jerks, exercise not pleasure.
The power of sex in us is very different.
Tenderness, gentleness, they're both built-in.

Sonnet: The Last Days

'Why have you put me here, underneath the earth?'
'You are still with us.'
'That cannot be. Beethoven is not here.'

– Schubert in delirium, during his last illness

When you lie in a hospital, in an old folks' home, in
                              your final illness,
all your defences are down. The brothers and sisters
                              you didn't get on with
can visit you at will. Sly women who expect legacies
can come and knit by your bedside, buttering you up.
Boring women with tactless talk of the deaths of
                              relatives –
the kind of friends you could do without – they all
                              swarm round you.
Even looking at them makes you tired, let alone
                              talking,
and you are scarcely protected by bossy nurses or
                              matrons.

If you are one of the distressed gentlefolk who live
                              into their nineties
in a fee-paying establishment, you'll find they take
                              furniture,
pinching a chair, a small cupboard (if you have such
                              things of your own),
a dishonest night-nurse will take any trinket of silver,
even the silver-framed small photo of a wife or a
                              husband.
Life must go on, they agree. If you can no longer see
                              them, what good are they to *you*?

PART THREE

A Pilgrimage

W.H. Auden (1907–73)

Wystan Hugh Auden, poet, was born in this house on
the 21st February 1907 – *inscription on 54 Bootham, York*

*Max: By the way, I forgot to tell you. There's one possible
     I saw yesterday, Mrs Stagg – the wife of the
     under-manager at Windyacre Mine. We might do
     worse. Vegery gegoegod bust.*
Ceslaus: Tegight cegunt?
*Max: I should think so. Her mouth's small enough,
     anyway.*

> – Fragment from *The Enemies of a Bishop*,
> unpublished play by Auden and Isherwood

Before you know quite where you are
you're standing there by Bootham Bar,
with handsome houses,
a now degraded road that feeds
traffic to Harrogate and Leeds,
a school that rouses

memories of one Cambridge friend*.
A.'s beginning is my end.
He started here,
Constance Rosalie gave out
a poet who was like a shout
and far and near

we clustered round to hear the Word
as clergymen ancestors deferred
to his new genius.
He put the thirties in their place,
Life hardly dared to show its face,
while like gardenias

* Frank Thistlethwaite, once at Bootham's School. The Auden
house is now one of the school buildings.

the lovely images were strown
in careless verses, quite full-blown,
bright in what's darker,
yet doomed, though serious and select,
to feel the Dracula Effect,
like Minna Harker.

The trouble of those old decades
before the telly and Teasmades!
He told of madness
deep in the body politic
(so right, though he himself was sick)
and all our sadness

whiffled down through those sensuous lines
where Western Decadence declines –
though, to speak truly,
much D.H. Lawrence nonsense too
was there to urge both me and you
to be unruly,

obey a Leader and take vows
while lovely women, those poor cows,
stayed strict at home.
(He made a U-turn of a sort
and finally came into port
not far from Rome.)

He was engaged once, married too,
and had a girlfriend he could screw,
but all his joys
lay in the arms of flaunting Chester
(a most notorious butch-molester)
and various boys.

Osborne and Carpenter declare
such doings as would raise the hair
on heads of Mormons –
if any lad has a wet dream
they beat him, naked, pray and scream –
what a performance!

He certainly gulped sex like food,
quite the reverse of any prude,
and, wholly greedy,
he wolfed huge helpings that he carved –
his cock was never stinted, starved,
or poor and needy.

That limestone landscape and those holes,
the lead mines that could save our souls –
a feminine body
and Mother's too, it seems to me.
There's not much else that it could be.
And, cute as Noddy,

he loved them and was never irked
although those mines were now not worked –
Dad's lust, I think,
was over, there was Mum, serene
and *his*; as though Dad hadn't been!
and with the ink

he poured such symbols, partly known,
into the poems. We should clone
not Dons or Wardens
but such eccentric bards as these
and make our bookish bread and cheese
from Wystan Audens.

The Peter Porter Poem of '82

This is going to be an ordinary friendly poem,
                              nothing very spectacular,
as it lollops along in the domain of what has been
                    called the republic of the vernacular.

Thirty years ago I first met you at a small party given
                              by Charles Rycroft –
but it wasn't until later that our paths became
                    brothers, like Sherlock and Mycroft.

At that time I had been more or less 'silent' for almost
                                        a quarter of a century
(as they say of poets) and the likely lads, in Faber
                                    fable, tough and adventury,

were Gunn and Hughes with their loonies in leather,
                                    rampageous pigs, cats, hawks,
all ready to murder you quickly; from lad- and
                Nature-lovers there were few protesting squawks.

You on the other hand were into the serious satirical
                                    Colonial-in-London bit,
lighting Latimer candles to Culture – and a good
                                        many candles were lit

by the best poems in that first book (*Once Bitten,
                                        Twice Bitten*),
which one could certainly call a very fine first book (if
                            not the best book ever written).

So we were into satire. Our London was brash,
                                    immoral, surprising –
'What a city to sack!' – it was sacked by advertising.

We met in pubs halfway between your civilized
                                agency and (much less so) mine.
Oh, there was literary laughter, and bottles and
                                        bottles of wine!

Later we both worked at Notley's – where no
                                highbrow had to grovel –
and I remember Trevor (with feminine help) xeroxing
                                        a whole novel.

'I see you're both working late', the Managing
                                        Director said
as he went off to his routine gins and tonics and
                                    dinner and bed.

'A nest of singing birds', Ewart, Porter and
                                    Lucie-Smith;
Oliver Bernard had gone before, creating a substantial
                                    Bohemian myth.

That satire rings truer now, in the money-mad world
                                    of a Thatcher,
and in the rye, alas, we're left without any catcher;

but writers, wrote Wystan (to Christopher?), are
                                    ironic points of light.
And I think you've certainly been one, before you go,
    and I go, and we all go into that not-so-good night.

A Little Musique in 1661

(See Samuel Pepys, *Diary*)

When twenties gramophones were tinny
and girls were shaking it in mini
immodest skirts
with bathroom gin, bootleggers, mobsters . . .
who knew that you *did eat two lobsters*
or cared? It hurts

to think how history behaves so flightily –
my head, you noted, *akeing mightily*
from *pints of wine*,
The Pillers of Hercules, *The Goate*
keeping your Navy men afloat –
where they could dine

on *chine of beef* and *leg of mutton*,
burnt-wine and *sack*, that every glutton
supped like a whale,
new-come-to-town North Country bugger
nine-pinned by *Rhenish wine and sugar*
or cups of ale!

They also gave some frightful wallops
to platters full of *eggs and collops*,
to eat an *udder*
was commonplace, although the thought
does not entice us as it ought,
but makes us shudder.

One friend did tell, and made *much sport*,
describing *his amours at Port-*
smouth to one
of Mrs Boates daughters; a kitten,
a pretty girl play of the Gitterne,
to hear – what fun!

In clover cloven hoof, hot pig!
So thinking there to *eat a wigg*
you late came home –
a dish of Anchoves gave you thirst,
fuddled perhaps, you never burst,
each chromosome

was *very merry with the ladies*,
though sermons gonged of Hell and Hades,
your *morning draught*
was standard, *barrels* too *of oysters*,
as *pickled* as old monks in cloisters,
both fore and aft,

kept you shipshape and in good case.
Your *flagelette* (and you sang bass)
was womanlike
in giving you and others pleasure;
good time, good tunes, proportions, measure,
no marlinspike

could separate melodic strands
(like piano pieces for eight hands)
when *ayres* were woven;
brave echo banged a bastinado,
opiniastrement, *rhodomontado*,
and pre–Beethoven!

Music was food – and you had cause
to love the art that Henry Lawes
practised divinely;
not reckoned by the frivolous, you
worked hard at what you had to do,
and did it finely.

NOTE Sack *is sherry,* burnt-wine *brandy,* collops *are
pieces of fried bacon, a* wigg *is a cake or bun. In the old
days people did actually burst from overeating. A* gitterne
is a kind of guitar, a flagelette *(flageolet) is an instrument
of the recorder family,* ayres *are tunes.* Opiniastrement *is
stubbornly (French),* rhodomontado *means a boast
(examples of Pepys' use of 'fashionable' words). Pepys was
very conscientious in his work for the Navy Office as well
as loving pretty women and music.*

Royal Hunt and Storm in Streatham ★

When a girl is on the bed
something's warm and wet and red.

Such inviting sights are seen
as delight the Paphian Queen.

One night-watchman never knew
until the age of sixty-two.

In those mystic Cyprian caves
the Mistress rules her willing slaves.

Vast the members and erect
she can with her rod correct.

★ Those to whom this poem seems obscure are advised to read *An
English Madam, The Life and Work of Cynthia Payne*, by Paul
Bailey (Jonathan Cape).

A Lesbic Thespian display
is the order of the day.

Exhibited, the cock will crow
in a slowly sensuous show.

Kinky letters in a host
rustle in by every post.

Some in cupboards grow more fond
of the strict restraining bond.

Dainty, feminine, soft lips
titillate the turgid tips.

Signor Dildo strictly stands,
urged by liver-spotted hands.

Nymph and Satyr change their dress
in venereal excess.

Leather vestments can excite,
and the flesh that Love may bite.

She is Queen, our Royal Madam,
Eve to fallen sons of Adam.

Rugger Song: The Balls of the Beaver

(Tune: 'Caviare Comes from the Virgin Sturgeon')

Castorium helpyth ayenst many Syknesses.

— Trevisa (1398)

The valuable drug Castoreum *is taken from the inguinal
glands of these animals. The antients had a notion it was
lodged in the testicles, and that the animal, when hard
pressed, would bite them off, and leave them to its pursuers,
as if conscious of what they wanted to destroy him for.*

— Pennant *History of Quadrupeds* (1781)

Castoreum comes from the balls of the Beaver –
Balls of the Beaver – very fine stuff!
A Beaver is truly a big deceiver –
And often found in a lady's muff!

Bothered Beavers will bite their balls off –
In that confusion they escape –
Huntsman checks his hunting – calls off
All that rowdiness and rape!

Now, I'm quite glad I'm not a Beaver –
Virile value's bad, you see!
It's my girlfriend – I can't leave her –
If I did a Beaver – she'd leave me!

The Pope and I

(Tune: 'The Sun Whose Rays' – *The Mikado*)

The Pope, whose face,
with robes and lace,
    brings such joy to the Faithful,
could never be
charisma-free
    or horrid, hard or scatheful!
Or hide his light
by day or night
    under a bush or bushel –
it will shine high
and reach the sky,
    proud as the Hindu Kush'll!

I mean to be *The* Bard
    before I die –
we really work quite hard,
    the Pope and I!

I've been on stage★
and on the page,
   and he has written plays too –
infallible
with every Bull,
   he's had his share of praise too!
No, we don't shrink
from printer's ink
   we're, each of us, a writer –
we share that crown
on field and town
   shines brighter than a mitre!

We're intellectual,
   we're no small fry,
we're truly on the ball,
   the Pope and I!

★ A one-act opera *Tobermory* (1979) with music by John Gardner.

It's the Songs

A Thirties Foxtrot

I'm a member of the Retrospect Collectors Society
and I collect old records as an act of piety –
I was playing a long-player of Rudy Vallee
(Twenty Suave Tracks By Yale's Golden Haired
                                        Crooner),
as bland and potent as a big sherry in a schooner,
he was the famous college boy bandleader of his day,
the *first* crooner (before Bing) if you don't count
                              Melville Gideon,
and he sang in the style that the old Greeks called the
                              Lydian . . .
I was sitting, typing to the music, when up came a
                                        track
that really took me back . . .

I was sixteen
at a summer East Coast cottage,
mooning to the soupy tune
from a very supportable
portable gramophone,
full of undistributed sex and quite alone . . .

It's the songs
from the days when you could dance
that remind you of romance,
how love was thought to be the righter of all
                                                    wrongs –
it's the songs!

It's the songs
that stir in you like yeast,
like a mystery from the East,
with the powerful unknown magic of Hawaiis and
                                                    Hong Kongs –
it's the songs!

Of course we'd heard of love –
was it beneath our notice or above?
Some wouldn't touch it (it was radioactive),
some moped and were romantic, some attractive
and very active . . .
there's nothing more confused, I'll wager,
than the average teenager!

It's the songs
remind you of an instinct
and the feelings that were sex-linked
as they beat in you like bonking tribal gongs –
it's the songs!

It's the songs
that infect you like the plague,
make you vaguer than a Haig –
once burned, you still don't handle them with tongs –
it's the songs!

It's the songs,
with their four beats to the bar,
no matter where you are,
that grip you firmly, as Fay Wray King Kongs –
it's the songs!

What innocence! we think,
what oceans still of neutral printer's ink,
typewriter fingers worn with calluses,
what years and further years spent in analysis
in Denvers, Dallases . . .
and love, from far unknown prehistory,
is still a magic and a mystery.

It's the songs –
how they still communicate
that highly charged emotive state,
mesmeric messages in Morse's shorts and longs!
It's the songs!

NOTE *The track referred to was 'The One in the World',
recorded 29 April 1929.*

De Quincey's Three Opium Dream Sonnets on the Wordsworth Family

1 Mrs Wordsworth

O Thou, so tall, so thin, with bean pole height –
Considerable obliquity of vision
Thou also hast, a squinting that Derision
Might too well claim would make a Left of Right!
Thine intellect not of an active order,
Thy only words, some say, a mere 'God bless you!'
For of thy Thoughts thou art a silent hoarder
And grave Philosophy would but distress you!
Thou art a Perfect Woman, nobly plann'd,
And few have seen so little of the World –
That once saw *Morecambe Bay's* extended sand –
In sweet confusion by a stranger hurl'd
Thou canst not speak, nay, colloquy would hurt you,
Dim burns thy Lamp of modest Female Virtue!

2 Dorothy Wordsworth

O rarely have I seen, among Eve's brood
Of English birth, a more determinate
And gipsy tan! Sweet, swarthy pigmy! Rude
Thou art not, and, though celibate
'Tis not from lack of courtship that thou holdest
A firm Companion to thy awesome Brother,
Thy babbling speech might well deter the boldest!
Thou cleav'st to Him, though woo'd by many
                                                another,
O'ercome entirely by thy winsome stammer!
Thy Suitors know thou art content to be
In ignorance of many things, to yammer
Or cry aloud in aid of Literacy
Not thine! Thy knowledge of the sacred cup
Was never systematically built up!

3 William Wordsworth

Great Wordsworth! Object of sublime devotion!
Thou walkest like a cade, an insect that
Obliquely wanders in its forward motion!
Thy legs are pointedly condemned – dog, cat
Walk better, cry the female connoisseurs!
Wry, twisted walking, and by slow degrees
Thou edgest off companions to the burrs
And gorse that hedge the high road's symmetries!
The worst part of thy person is thy Bust,
All from the shoulders narrowness and droop,
That give effects of Meanness! Ah, too just
The sculptor's disapproval of thy stoop!
Dorothy walks behind thy crablike crooks:
'Can that be William? How very mean he looks!'

NOTE   *These sonnets are based on De Quincey's writings on Wordsworth and the Lake Poets. A 'cade' is a dialect name for a kind of insect that cannot walk straight.*

Edward and I

We guard the pillow on your bed,
                    Edward and I,
and keep it ready for your head,
                    Edward and I.
The nightdress hangs there on the door,
the fur-trimmed slippers on the floor
expect those feet that we adore,
                    Edward and I!

While I in thought and he in fact,
                    Edward and I,
are guardians, we have made a pact,
                    Edward and I,

to stay there always, each a sentry,
and (though we die!) deny all entry
to the lewd lords, degenerate gentry –
                    Edward and I!

The bed by day, the chair's long nights,
                    Edward and I
share with bedspreads, panties, tights.
                    Edward and I,
jumbled with stockings, slips and bras,
reflect on drinkers flushed from bars.
We know the dangers of fast cars,
                    Edward and I!

Like medicine men who point the bone,
                    Edward and I
can hex admirers, we alone
                    (Edward and I)
remind you not to swing a breast
or lift a leg for any guest –
we are the loved ones, not the rest,
                    Edward and I!

Combined, we keep you from such harm,
                    Edward and I,
I – spirit! He – the secular arm!
                    Edward and I
are dedicated to your worship,
and death to dirty dogs and curship;
we sing this hymn to your sweet Hership,
                    Edward and I!

NOTE   *Edward is a small Edward Gorey cat, stuffed with
beads.*

A Word to the Wise

. . . one of Britain's naughtiest and most popular poets.

– The Good Book Guide

A good many poets are haughty,
despising the unlettered mass,
but *we* know it pays to be *naughty*
(the way of a lad with a lass

is always attractive to readers) –
that's where popularity lies,
with the old fast reaction sex breeders
and the explicit bosoms and thighs!

No poet can be a best seller
unless he's an expert on hair,
like a forkbending straight Uri Geller –
getting rich as his writing gets rare;

and everything raw, wet and steamy
makes readers in thousands enthuse,
Mack, Mick, and Matilda and Mimi
are moaning aloud at his Muse!

Oh, the critics may say 'contrapuntal'
and write of his verbal technique
but unless it is all fully frontal
it's as dull as a very wet week!

Verse may be symbolic or Sapphic,
and written with wonderful words
but unless it makes love photographic
it's strictly, *we* know, for the birds!

You may boast of your spondees and trochees,
your rhyme royal and your villanelle –
it's the love dances, hot hokey-cokeys,
stop it getting as boring as hell!

And that's why each sly sexy oldie
is so keen to flash and to spank –
though at heart he is mean, mild and mouldy,
it's all money (you bet!) in the bank!

Beryl's Poem

In the old days when Abraham was sacrificing Thing
not many of the Jews could have a little jump out.
All the concubines belonged to the patriarchs.

Many claimed God had given them permission.
Women taken in adultery were stoned
with real stones, not whisky on the rocks.

It was a rough ride. No cart ever had a spring.
The Lion of Judah could bite quite a big lump out.
Couples were rare, as rare as Noah's arks.

Onan was punished for his lonely emission.
Desire reached a very sharp point – well honed.
But only the Holy Men had hens to match their cocks. .

'Came Away with Betjeman to Pull Him Along Through Wulfstan Until Dinner Time'

– C.S. Lewis' Diary (1927)

Come away, Betjeman! Pull for the shore!
Pull on through Wulfstan and anglo that sax!
This is the tune that entices us more
Than vernal Vaughan Williams or beautiful Bax!
We can be happy, so happy, we twain,
With liege-lord and serf and intransigent thane!

Come away, Betjeman! Mince down the High,
Think not of Wystan or sorbets or sex!
Drink not the wine, of the neatherd's young thigh
All the enchantment can only perplex!
Plain living, high thinking – of such there's a dearth,
We'll raise it and praise it on our Middle Earth!

NOTE *At Oxford University in 1927 C.S. Lewis was
John Betjeman's Tutor. Lewis regarded him as a hopeless
young aesthete, and his attempts to interest him in
Anglo-Saxon seem to have ended in failure.*

Lincoln Kirstein: Rhymes of a PFC

In an Art Nouveau pizzeria
I thought about Lincoln's book
and restaurants called *Da Zia*
from when I took my first look
at Italy, wilder and freer
than any Tour with Cook –

for we came in at Gragnano,
Christmas 1943,
and worked our way up to the Arno
and right to the top of the tree,
mens sana in corpore sano,
La Spezia! Fiddle-de-dee,

we weren't those combat fighters!
Just air defence of ports
and airfields! But detritus
we weren't, or out of sorts,
and we were quite as bright as
those young heroic sports

who bought it at Anzio, easily
the worst FU of the war –
we turned up there later, queasily
surveying the tragic spoor
of the great hot beast. Oh, weaselly
we slid in under the door!

Not terribly efficient,
I was an officer then –
but I started to get proficient
among the enlisted men –
the drill was more than sufficient,
not to mention the Bren!

You think you know about stripping –
just try stripping a gun!
The Bren and the Bofors are ripping
and furious fast-thinking fun.
In summer the sweat starts dripping,
in winter your hands are numb . . .

Let me entreat your cold ear!
I was a Private too,
a blinking bob-a-day soldier
(that's twenty cents to you)
but still an immortal soul, dear,
if Padres tell us true –

conscripted, the old East Surreys,
with NCOs from the Raj
who put us in several hurries
and knew their butter from marge –
the cookhouse even served curries!
Our ignorance was large,

the square was there for the bashing
and France was folding up,
June 1940. For mashing,
some swedes★ were holding up

★ Cockney slang for rustics.

the whole effing issue, not dashing
but slow as a loving-cup,

they were the bleeding Dorsets,
all hating it, farmer's boys
old-fashioned as grandma's corsets,
and drill wasn't one of their joys –
a Sergeant, a practical whore, sets
high standards for virgins and coys . . .

At least I can say sincerely
(like thousands) that I was there,
more clever than brave and more nearly
the tortoise than any young hare –
but I loved my life quite dearly
(a thing that isn't so rare).

The US Army Air Force! Boy,
I was attached to them once!
Don't signal it out in old Morse, boy,
or foul it all up like a dunce –
that breakfast! a true assault course, boy,
(such hunter comes back to, who hunts)!

Pup tents and ice cream and chow lines
and movies and combat boots –
I knew them. Each war book that now lines
my shelves – I'm right there at the roots,
in the mud. War, like a sacred cow, lines
us up for these deadly pursuits!

So it's gone, and we go, but a witness
to what they suffered is fit
and Kirstein's verse has a fitness,
to humour the horror with wit,
to pinpoint its actual itness –
the glory, the shame, the shit.

Love in a Valley ★

Valkyrie's Valspeak in Awesome Valhalla

I used to think Wotan was vicious
in all that gear, a real soc, a mega hunk

We flew high, a bitchen sesh,
it was radical!

Those pointy things on his helmet
were truly gnarly, the Heinies were
tubular.
And the Lowies.

Totally!

The bud was caj
we scarfed out. It was hot.
He maxed OK

OK!
How come he get so gross?
such a zod, so nerdy?
a shanky spaz?

OK!
Now I wanta say:

Gag me with a spoon!
What a geek!
You were mondo cool
but now you're grody
you make me barf
you're not buf any more . . .

★ Spoken, as it were, by a Valley Girl in Los Angeles, living in or
near the San Fernando Valley.

Oh my God!
Kiss my tuna!
What a nerd!
Get away!
Your fat butt disgusts me!

MS Found in a Victorian Church★

Golly! Let's debag old Kingers!
What a brilliant thought!
One of our most King Size singers!
Praise him as we ought –
That would be extremely hard!
But still we'll jolly well teach him
To be a Bard!

Though we love him daily, nightly,
Calling people shags
Is the fault that very rightly
Makes him lose his bags!
To respect his fellow men –
That idea may some day reach him
And his pen!

Flying tackles are in order,
Grab him round the waist,
Hold him hard South of the Border,
Give him quite a taste
Of the fate of sods and pseuds
When they bow down and beseech him
In their feuds!

★ Thought to be a poem by Sir John Betjeman about Kingsley
Amis, but the presence of another hand has been suspected.

Let him know the harsh unzipping,
The outcome of the knees!
Violence is simply ripping –
Down his Y-fronts, please!
Gosh! We've got him! Chewing gum out!
In unmentionable places bleach him,
Scream and shout!

A Soft Spot for Him – and Her

(A Night Club Song)

Once Bach wrote an Air on the G String
before it was used by the dancers –
who hid pubic hair with a G-string,
as was known in Las Vegas and Kansas;
then the thirties invented the G-Man, a new kind of
man,
and in Britain they'd furniture once that was labelled
G-Plan.
But now, red-hot and sparkling new,
the G-spot comes to you!

O the G-spot
is a wee spot
penny-size but more than / penny-wise
on the front wall of the vagina
and active from Chichester to China!

O the G-spot
is a free spot,
not ashamed before your / very eyes
to glory in ejaculation
and stand erect – with proper titillation!

O very bitter is
the lot of the clitoris,
quite in disgrace
it hides its face –
outdistanced by this famous female spasm
that gives to girls their final
vaginal orgasm!

O the G-spot
is a she-spot,
it's so great that it could / win a prize
and it's truly hidden treasure,
and glad to be there for one purpose – pleasure!

The Heel Has Come Full Circle

Old Mugg has come home,
he's truly done roamin',
he's homed in to Rome,
old Mugg has come home
to where he was homin',

St Peter's great dome
has changed his religion –
sanctimonious gnome
(what a gnome, what a dome!)
and religion's his pigeon,

like Venus from foam
he appears, that great actor,
like a sage with a tome,
full of faith, froth and foam
and a sick-making factor!

106

A McGonagall-type Triolet on the Full Revoltingness of Commercial Fast Food

A great double-deck of pure beef with melting cheese,
　　　　　　　pickle, ketchup and mustard!
Complete your meal with our crisp French Fries and a
　　　　　　　cool thick Shake!
Enjoy too the fried jumbo-size jumbo-tough
　　　　　　　breadcrumbed macho legs of the Bustard,
a great double-deck of pure beef with melting cheese,
　　　　　　　pickle, ketchup and mustard,
with a few lightly boiled rats' foetuses on the side, all
　　　　　　　masked in creamy custard!
Wash it down with a warm Guinness, topped up with
　engine oil – and dunk in it our supermale Elephant Cake,
a great double-deck of pure beef with melting cheese,
　　　　　　　pickle, ketchup and mustard!
Complete your meal with our crisp French Fries and a
　　　　　　　cool thick Shake!

NOTE　*The first two lines of this poem are genuine food advertising of March 1984 in a London take-away/eat-in restaurant.*

The Dugong

(Lewis Carroll Watches Television)

That dugong looked so deadly sweet,
　it lay there and it looked
like something very good to eat,
　just waiting to be cooked.

I thought I heard its spirit speak:
　'They drown us when we're caught,
for they are strong and we are weak
　and life is very fraught!

And soon we shall be quite extinct –
   the experts say ten years.
This statement's true, although succinct.'
   It then burst into tears.

'With outboard motors and canoes
   they chase us on the reefs.
We're on the menu, though they choose
   to hold some odd beliefs.

They think echidnas are our mums
   and ancestors of old.
They roast us, with the beating drums,
   we're valuable as gold –

part of their import-export trade,
   related, too, to *man* –
this claim the priestly ones have made
   since rituals began.

With sympathetic magic too
   they try to hunt us down.
It makes us very bored and blue
   as any girl's blue gown!'

I heard the mild and murdered beast.
   My mouth was full of veal.
I wasn't troubled in the least –
   it looked a perfect meal!

NOTE *The natives of Papua New Guinea are engaged in hunting the dugong or sea cow to extinction. They believe that the things of the sea can never be exhausted. The programme that Lewis Carroll watched was a David Attenborough programme: 'The Kiwai – Dugong Hunters of Daru'. A certain hardness, and even sadism, can be found in Carroll's poetry (see 'The Mouse's Tale' in* Alice in Wonderland).

Evil Girl Guide in Torture Horror

EVIL GIRL GUIDE IN TORTURE HORROR –
Ordeal of Mabel, 75.
You wouldn't read about it in Gomorrah
(Evil Girl Guide in Torture Horror)!
Sue (18) and her simple-minded lover – two sadist
                              Japs crying *Torah! Torah!*
Cigarette-burns salt-rubbed, clothes-pegged eyes, a
plastic carnation stuck up her nose, rat-bitten,
indecently assaulted with a toilet brush,
laxative-overdosed, robbed, regarded as an easy con,
was Mabel lucky to be alive?
EVIL GIRL GUIDE IN TORTURE HORROR –
Ordeal of Mabel, 75.

NOTE   *The first two lines of this triolet are headlines from*
The Sun *of 24 March 1984; and, as in poems by Peter*
Reading, the facts are true ones, as given in that paper's
account of the trial.

A Wee Sang for the Tourists

Come my Lords and Lieges, let us all to dinner for the
Cock-a-Leekie is a cooling.

   – James VI of Scotland (on a Baxter's Soup Label)

Och! I long for yon Auld Reekie,
where they're drinkin' Cock-a-Leekie
                              soup,
where the lassies are sae musky,
a' the better for a whusky-
                              stoup!

Where the pipes are busy skirlin'
and the kilts are wild an' whirlin'
                              wide –
where the music's like a fountain,
Arthur's sittin' on a mountain-
                              side!

Embro Toun's nae warm Devonian
an' she's no a Caledonian
                              Hell –
cauld an' in nae over-hot land,
the bra pride o' Bonnie Scotland –
                              swell!

Tourist Guides say she's romantic
an' they cross the great Atlantic,
                              glad
tae see clear what made Burns sary
an' yon tragic Queen, Scots Mary,
                              sad!

Edinburgh Rock! Identic-
ally, like the Mound, authentic
                              Scots!
An' nae matter what your mood is
the Past Appeal o' Holyrood is
                              lots!

John Knox, Stevenson, Sir Walter –
History wad surely falter
                              if
names like these cam off the roster,
nane o' them is an impostor!
                              Syph

an' a' disease unmentionable
(they wadna live on tae a pensionable
                              age)
got a hauld on th'auld Scots Lords!
houghmagandie-lovin' sots! Lords!
                              Sage,

we forget sic things an' Mary's
Bothwell, Darnley shine like fairies
                              nou!
Fine auld Lady o' the Lake-rid,
come to Embro, Scotland's sacred
                              cou!

The Mating of Pseudoscorpions

British Pseudoscorpions. *Fertilization is effected by
means of a spermatophore, which in pseudoscorpions consists
of a small rod bearing a globule of seminal fluid at the top.
It is deposited by the male during the course of an elaborate
nuptial dance, etc., etc.*

– Information display in the British Museum (Natural
  History). Pseudoscorpions are only a few millimetres
                                            long.

Pseuds and pseudopoets mating!
Long displays worth celebrating
in the most elaborate verses!
Kids' play, Doctors and pert Nurses!
Barings of the bum and tit you all
know is true poetic ritual –
an Editor can show his sonnet,
she can nymphlike dance upon it –
not spirits only that she raises,
as caressingly she praises!
In a wine bar, dark and smoky,
he can stun her with a trochee,
initiates are into mysteries
you won't find in Natural Histories . . .

Pubs are Forests of green Arden,
where Odes To A Surrey Garden
melt hearts and parts of young aspirants
and Editors are forceful tyrants –

they're locks in which they'll make their keys stick
with Eng. Lit. love that's anapaestic!

Spermatophores are simple lyrics
where landscapes lie in panegyrics.
He will drop them. Vestals hover
above that seminal spot of bother.
Fertilization! Consummation!
Pseudopoets of the Nation,
with their magazines and readings,
pseudoscorpions' dancelike pleadings,
flicker-flames that don't light fuses,
are dear to all hearts – but the Muse's!

The Pilgrim's Progress

In the City that men called Destruction
there were riot, rebellion and ruction –
all around was depraved –
Christian longed to be saved,
and Evangelist gave him instruction:

Go ahead to that old Wicket Gate –
forget Pliable's, Obstinate's fate!
Cross the Slough of Despond
(it's a Doubt-ridden pond)
to Celestial City, old mate!

Worldly-Wiseman, and his pal Legality,
were diversions. But in that locality
Good Will helped him through.
Past the Gate, what was new
was Interpreter's pictured morality . . .

At the Cross, next, his Burden fell off.
But the Sinners were still there to scoff –
dopey Simple and Sloth,
and he passed by them both,
and Hypocrisy (big-headed toff).

Still, the Shining Ones gave him a boost,
and a Roll which he frequently used.
Difficulty (a Hill)
at first made him ill.
There were lions on chains (but not loosed).

And then Prudence, Piety, Charity
gave him discourse, without much hilarity;
they were virgins, of course,
a benevolent force.
One was dark, one was blonde, one was carrotty.

So next day he went down with elation,
to the Valley called Humiliation –
(the Delectable Mountains,
with fruit, flowers and fountains,
had been shown him, a strong inspiration).

WHAM! BAM! Up the creek with no paddle!
A foul fiend there, astride and astraddle,
my gosh and by golly! On
the path stands Apollyon
(says Salvation is all fiddle-faddle)!

Then fierce combat ensued (half a day)
till the fiend dragon's-winged on his way!
Chris had hardly drawn breath
when the Shadow of Death
stretched its Valley before him, okay?

Full of Hobgoblins, Dragons and Satyrs,
howling, yelling, and other such matters,
with clouds of Confusion
in darkening profusion,
and fiends that could tear him to tatters.

But his Sword and All-Prayer got him through,
past quags, gins, nets, traps – Pagan too
and Pope, two great Giants
both breathing defiance.
They were all there, lined up in a queue!

So he overtook Faithful quite soon,
who gave out about Wanton's sex-tune,
how he steadfastly went,
braving Pride, Discontent
and false Shame. Pilgrim songs, to the moon,

they both sang – and passed Talkative by.
Next it's Vanity Fair, my, oh, my!
All fashions, all vogues,
cheats, games, whores and rogues!
They seem simple, where others are sly . . .

So, arrested and put in a cage,
chained and beaten, with malice and rage,
they speak fair, no denial –
but they must stand trial.
Lord Hategood is Judge, that bent sage!

They are charged that they, mean and penurious,
scorned Lords Carnal Delight and Luxurious,
Lord Old Man and Lord Lechery –
to Beelzebub treachery!
So Lord Hategood gets perfectly furious.

In fact Faithful is tortured and burned,
eternal Redemption thus earned,
with angels and bliss.
Now Hopeful finds Chris.
They march on and will never be turned

by the twerps that in Fair-speech abound.
Lady Faining, Mr By-ends, are found,
Mr Smooth-man (Mr Any-Thing's
at home with too many things).
Mr Facing-bothways is around.

The Plain is called Ease; the Hill, Lucre –
it's a lot like a long game of snooker.
Rest from mayhem and slaughter,
by the stream of the Water
of Life, it's a cool Poulaphouca★!

★ a waterfall in Eire.

Doubting Castle, its lord Giant Despair,
are the next things of which they're aware.
There are no surprises;
suicide, he advises,
is the way to get out of his hair!

Next he shows them the bones of the slain
and, for good luck, he beats them again.
'We're a couple of dummies!
This key that's called Promise
will relieve us' cries Chris, 'from our pain!'

So it's off to Delectable Mountains –
gardens, orchards, and vineyards and fountains –
it's Immanuel's Land,
shepherds give them a hand.
Mountains Error and Caution! Past countings

and reckonings, by-ways to Hell
are all round, with a brimstony smell.
But they climb up and peer
from a Hill that's called Clear –
there's the City, as clear as a bell!

Still Faint-heart, Mistrust and one Guilt
frighten Little-faith up to the hilt,
seven devils get Turn-away.
It's hard to discern a way,
but at last they're off, no blood is spilt –

and they're netted by Flatterer next,
a specious ungodly mar-text.
Now they're set for Mount Sion,
as bold as a lion,
though by Turn-back and Ignorance vexed.

Through the River of Death, the last thing,
and the Shining Ones' trumpets all ring!
That melodious noise
tells us all of the joys
of the Pilgrims who sing with their King!

The Inventor of Franglais?

A Comment

Thence to Jervas's, my mind, God forgive me, running too much after sa fille, but elle not being within, I away by coach to the Change – and thence home to dinner; and finding Mrs. Bagwell waiting at the office after dinner, away elle and I to a cabaret where elle and I have été before; and there I had her company toute l'après-diner and had mon plein plaisir of elle – but strange, to see how a woman, notwithstanding her greatest pretences of love à son mari and religion, may be vaincue.

– Samuel Pepys, *Diary (23 January 1665)*

Well, God, j'ai souvent pensé
(in clear or fractured français),
a pris the soul of femmes –
but toutefois the Devil maudit
is souverain of their body
and has his will of Dames!

He does all that he voulait
to each partridge or poulet,
we're instruments – c'est tout!
Bon Dieu, above, has thunder –
le Diable rules what's under –
très bon for me and you!

Les female protestations
qui annoncent their detestations
of all luxurieux men
sont for the record only,
le corps stays soft and lonely
et le fait again and again!

The Importance of Being Earnest

Jack Worthing is free, fit and fine –
and he knows about women and wine.
Less coarse than a sandbag,
he was found in a *handbag* –
on the Brighton, that famous old line.

Algy Moncrieff does a Bunbury
to places like Paris or Sunbury –
to see a sick friend
who is nearing his end –
but in truth he's at Joysville or Funbury!

There are two girls: Gwendolen, Cecily,
who go round full of wit, and quite dressily.
Lady Bracknell's the Aunt –
not her fault that it shan't
end in tears and in all ways quite messily!

C.'s governess, prune-faced Miss Prism,
Canon Chasuble; heresy, schism
fly away when *he's* there.
She'd be willing to share
any fate as his mate – cataclysm!

Now Jack's told one lie or another,
told Cecily he has a brother
called Ernest – who's wicked –
this isn't quite cricket
(no one knows yet who might be his mother).

So the Albany country-house lads
must endure the girls' maidenly fads –
C.'s a chick who in *her* nest
wants no one not Ernest.
Ditto Gwendolen. *Christen us cads!*

is the favour they both of them ask,
it's the Canon's canonical task.
But – one last catechism –
Lady B. questions Prism,
and the Truth is revealed, with no mask!

That (how fateful and how well-arranged!)
for a *novel* the young Jack was changed
by Miss Prism, his nurse,
and for better or worse
he's the brother of Alg., long estranged!

Even better, his true given name
will revive the young Cecily's flame!
For it's Ernest (no catch!),
so it's game, set and match
(and the winner was wit in that game)!

An Easy Lai?★

But is it very hard?
Ah! Why not ask the Bard?
   He's the one who knows.
He's wily, he's a card,
a fryer without lard,
   to whom each ill wind blows

some straw; invention grows,
his bricks pile up in rows –
   all of them make the grade!
Though critics stand like crows,
crying down his furbelows,
   saying spade should be a spade,

★ This is, in fact, the hardest kind of lai (a medieval French form of obscure origin) known as the *virelai ancien*.

he surely has it made.
Although his talents fade,
   his lines like spikenard
smell sweet – or marmalade –
like cleverly carved jade
   they merit our regard!

A Wordsworthian Sonnet for Arnold Feinstein, who Mended My Spectacles in Yugoslavia

Feinstein, artificer of proven worth!
O Saviour of my spectacles! Thou didst know
Exactly where that tiny screw should go
And how to place it there! Of all on earth
I honour thee! Of such men there is dearth –
Great Scientists that yet will stoop so low,
To rude *Mechanics*! Our Life cannot show
A truer Nobleness, or of such pure birth!
Yet thou, by Struga, in that moving coach,
Spinoza-like didst work upon the lens
With aptitude more great than other men's,
Reintroducing it! O dread approach
Of bookish blindness! From which I was set free
When Fate ordained that thou sat'st next to me!

Happiness is Girl-Shaped

(The Copywriter Sings)

You're twice as trad as Acker Bilk,
you'd be delicious
                crumbled into milk,
there is no other of your ilk!

You're very clearly bran-enriched,
I'd like to have you
                    hedged and ditched,
no hype for you is over-pitched!

My heart, for you, has raced like Arkle,
you've got that cute
                    refreshing sparkle,
you are my light that will not darkle!

You have that tangy lemon zest,
great things have happened
                    on your chest,
you're way out there beyond the rest!

You make life bright and dazzling new,
you are the first
                    of precious few,
I'd like to have a private view!

You set me off like fire alarms,
persuasive as
                    a salesman's charms,
I'd make down payments on your arms!

You are the rhyme that's always true,
the whitest wash
                    that's slightly blue –
let me consume my life with you!

Rush That Bear!

There's a breathless hush over Crescent and Square
    and the Gardens are sad and still
    while everybody, yes, everywhere,
    wonders: Will
Sir John go over the hill?

The agonized cry goes up: *Rush that bear*
to his grieving, tormented side!
This is the comfort, in his despair,
far and wide
all wish for him, tearful-eyed!

This is the single much-more-than-toy
that can succour him in his need –
Archibald, seventy years of joy,
of joy indeed,
as Venerable as Bede!

So take him by taxi, by tube or by train,
fly him so high in the air!
Give us some hope, let us breathe again
(oh, if we dare!)
and speedily RUSH THAT BEAR!

NOTE   *In October 1983 Sir John Betjeman suffered a heart*
attack and his childhood teddy bear, Archibald, was brought
to his hospital bed.

Two Kiplings

1 Sixty-seven and going West

When your hair gets thin and your tummy expands
and the frog-spots play all over your hands,
when benign skin-cancers cover your back
and warts, all over, are on the attack –
why, then you'll know (if you haven't guessed)
that you're sixty-seven and going West!

When your face gets fat with a jowly jaw
and your teeth feel like a neglected saw,
when your legs walk easily into cramp,
and your eyes grow tired in the reading lamp –
why, then you'll know (if you haven't guessed)
that you're sixty-seven and going West!

When you feel arthritis in finger-ends
and the stiffness of Death lays out your friends,
when the hand writes wobbly and memory goes
and your hearing weakens, from head to toes
you'll have the *proof* (if you haven't guessed)
that you're sixty-seven and going West!

2 John Kipling

(posted missing in 1915, aged seventeen)

Warned against women, he went off to war,
Dad's most treasured cub in the whole Wolf Pack,
Abraham's Isaac – but where was the ram?

Trained to kiss rods, to kiss and adore,
He never would blub, he was white, not black,
He had a little bread – but never any jam.

A Small Elite

(George Macbeth and I)

We can both say 'I'm a genius'
(since it all depends what you mean by genius)
though to misspellers we might be henious★
crimes –
a huge claim made by tiny, teeny us!
But still, at times,

we have 'touch' like Gerulaitis
(with the skill of Gower or Gerulaitis) –
for those who speak of arthuritis
we
are see-through frauds like certain nighties.
A different key

★ or even Heaneyous

122

is what we play in – and *hoi polloi*ing
(all the screaming screamers, *hoi polloi*ing)
masses would find us quite annoying
pseuds –
since Pop is what they're all enjoying,
and genteel nudes.

I thank you that you called me Scottish
(never skilled like Burns but truly Scottish),
though horrorpots are horrorpottish
it's
quite nice to know not all are sottish –
a cap that fits

we share, though we're South of the Border
(in exile both for certain, South of the Border)
where they rhyme this with Harry Lauder
and
we're hounded by each out-of-order
analysand!

A Happy Encounter at a Literary Function

(Tune: A simplified version of the song in *High Noon*)

What blazered arm lay on my shoulder?
    Say, was it Laurence, of the Cott'rell clan?
As I must die (and burn or moulder)
    I can't deny it was that very man!

And I was more than glad to see him!
    A welcome rainbow, from the sun and rain!
To toast him, wine him, or high-tea him
    Would be a pleasure keen as best champagne!

For from the Compton Fund the money
    Lay on us through his efforts truly great!
If we were crumpets, this was honey –
    And proved him, ev'ry inch, a genuine mate!

Craig Raine and I, and Dr Dannie Abse
   Were in New York then, with Patricia Beer,
Where Laurence, Fairy Queen and quite Queen
                                          Mabsy,
   Kept us in funds and truly free from fear!

Britain Salutes New York! That was the message!
   He *managed* us! The Pickwick Arms Hotel!
Like horses that step orderly in dressage
   He led us round that circus very well!

And now some *fees* are paid for readings,
   And we know well to whom our thanks are due!
To you, dear Laurence, and your pleadings!
   Only and always, from us four to you!

Life in Scotland, 1852

Neighbours are landladies
landladies are neighbours
and their speech is in the street,

wee complaints are colloquies
colloquies are wee complaints
on their steadfast Scottish feet,

miners are miseries,
miseries are miners,
but their coal provides the heat,

tempers are open fires,
open fires are tempers,
when the bold landladies meet!

Blue Maggie

(Red Ken's Song)

She isn't saggy, she isn't baggy,
she's quite inconceivable, her hair's unbelievable,
Blue Maggie!
Of course she cares! (if it's Stocks and Shares),
she's not quite real, as slim as an eel, and truly
                                              genteel,
Blue Maggie!

She's full of friction, she's Science Fiction,
she's extra-terrestrial, bimetallic, bimestrial,
Blue Maggie!
She never defers to ideas not hers,
she's quite absolute, and resolute, and mad as a coot,
Blue Maggie!

A Ballad Re-Creation of a Fifties Incident at Barnes Bridge

'Tis the ghost o' Colquhoun an' the ghost o' McBride
That do balcony-lean by yon auld riverside,
An' they baith are sae fou' they can scarcely see –
For they're baith at a party (where booze is free) –

An' the Sassenachs there wi' their highbrowish
                                              speech
Mak' a nebulous nectarine oot o' a peach.
But Colquhoun an' McBride hauld theirsels weil
                                              aloof,
Aye drinkin' the drinks that are ower proof.

Nae word do they speak, but they lean an' glower
Wi' the pissed perfection o' painterly power –
An' as they lean there the sun gaes doun
Like a watercolour o'er London toun,

In a' the sweet tints that the calendars love,
Wi' a braw great pink flush i' the skies above.
Och! they *do* notice this, tho' their eyes are glazed,
An' baith wi' horror are sair amazed –

Colquhoun turns tae McBride wi' a fine disgust
At the sight o' that distant an' reddenin' dust.
'Mon, but it's horrible!' 'Aye, but 'twill pass!'
An' they ply, baith, the gold, unremittin' wee glass!

NOTE   *This haunting is quite a possible one, being based
on an actual incident. Colquhoun and McBride were two
painters of talent from Glasgow, well-known in the forties
and fifties.*

False Colours

Everybody's heard of the young man in London
who went round seducing American girl students
by telling them he was Ted Hughes . . .

I bet he was only *one* of them –
I bet in Northern Ireland there are pseudo-Heaneys,
imitation Betjemans active in Metroland,
false Roy Fullers stroking a lustful moustache
before the proud beauties,
in the North perhaps a deutero-Geoffrey Hill,
a Bunting wrapped in some deceptive skin.
All men of foresight and acumen, telling the tale.

126

There will be, too, a few rather queerer seductions
engineered by Americans posing as Thom Gunn,
scholars disguised as John Heath-Stubbs . . .
the kids in Cornwall must beware the cater-Causley.

And a good many Fleur Adcocks must be drawing
                                    the young men in,
there's probably a Patricia Beer operating in Devon,
and a doubtful Maureen Duffy.

All students everywhere must be terribly careful!

A Godly Undertaking

I continually pray for the SOU-
L of the novelist Evelyn Waugh.
It seems dark and obscure, half a MO-
LE, and unfriendly and raw.

It didn't much like fellow-ME-
N, it was snobbish and cruel to the weak,
and it harmed what he wrote with his PE
N and the words it induced him to speak.

It took sides, where it could, with the STRO-
NG and all privilege led it astray.
It's in Hell, I expect (am I WRO-
NG?) – that's why I so steadfastly pray!

British Weather

It is the merry month of May,
when everything is cold and grey,
the rain is dripping from the trees
and life is like a long disease,

the storm clouds hover round like ghouls,
the birds all sing, because they're fools,
and beds of optimistic flowers
are beaten down by thunder showers,

under a weak and watery sun
nothing seems to be much fun –
exciting as a piece of string,
this is the marvellous British Spring!

Under the Staircase

(For Several Voices)

Semi-Chorus A: Under the staircase
under the stair
you won't find anything rich and
        rare –
things more likely
that shouldn't be there,
a china pisspot brimming full,
emu's eggs in cotton wool,
things that are scary,
sad or sinister –
the strangled body
of the Prime Minister!

Semi-Chorus B: Never look
under the stair,
oh, have a care!
Hanks of hair
and bones all knobbly
lie in wait like an old nightmare –
to make you weak and wobbly!
The hacked-off head
of a grizzly bear –
don't look, don't look,
even for a dare,
under the stair!

Semi-Chorus A:	It isn't a rare case,
	it isn't rare
	to find a Something lurking there –
	to stare you out
	with its horrible stare –
	something mouldy, mad and
	moulting,
	infantile and quite revolting!
	Hedgehogs squashed
	on the highway camber,
	kittens in creosote,
	frogs in amber!

Semi-Chorus B:	Never look
	under the stair!
	Foul, not fair,
	Baudelaire
	in Vicky squalor
	lies embalmed with a poxed *au*
	pair,
	with ink-stink on his collar!
	Better be dead
	than stoop and peer –
	don't look, don't look,
	it's bad, it's bare
	under the stair!

The Mistress

A Betjeman Rewrite★

There's lust in the beds of London
(and he is a husband surely)
and love in the beds of London
(and she is a wife, or nearly);

★ The poem to which the reader is referred is 'Lenten Thoughts
Of A High Anglican'

there are evening beds in London
(and wives and mistresses share them)
and afternoon beds in London
(the charms, legs and arms, they bare them).

There's love and there's lust in London
(to separate them's not easy)
and The Mistress is great in London
(and the appetite isn't queasy).

And this is the way in London
(underground love – like travel),
there's knotting and play in London
(that only Time can unravel)!

Fairly High Windows

(based on an idea of Vernon Scannell's)

They fuck you up, your King and Queen.
  They may not mean to, but they do.
And things that are no way your scene
  All have to be extolled by you.

They have a strict and soppy code
  That never bends much or relents.
Each Royal Birth's a fucking Ode
  And camp as any row of tents.

The Laureate misery's handed down,
  Letters from fools too, sack by sack.
You have to wear that iron crown.
  You're not allowed to give it back.

NOTE *Written in expectation of Philip Larkin achieving the Laureateship, June 1984.*

End of Term, 23 July

I offer you the salmon trout of kindness
and Edward from his bed approves the gift;
in this I serve, like Milton in his blindness,
this is the gold that daily diggers sift,

the cloud-based and proverbial silver lining
that hangs around our ordinary life,
the precious metal some say needs refining,
the help of husbands to a working wife.

The loganberries will appear, quite *glacé*,
enrobed in mystical, pure, Single Cream,
the fridge-freed wine will be a *Royal Crustacé*,
a *blanc de blancs*, a draught that's like a dream.

The chocolates come from *Charbonnel et Walker*,
each catalogued as any champion cat.
Marrow and new potatoes! No trick talker
could better this, or make a meal like that!

Lexicography

(A Trough of Low Pleasure)

Like a lepidopterist with a fine new specimen
Carried carefully home from a successful sortie,
What did I do with this marvellous trophy?
   Spread it out and put it under the microscope!

This, the *OED* in its Compact Edition,
Carried a reading glass, a standard extra.
What did I search for? Just like anyone,
   Looked up CUNT, to see it under the reading glass

(The same would have been done by the magazine
                                                    editors
And by all the publishers, including Virago,
It's an important word and basic in folklore,
    Known about and spoken, over the hemispheres),

Keats' friends drank to it as Mater Omnium, ,
It's full of sexual overtones and sensual undertones,
It has a kind of inwardness that some call mystical.
    So I crept, so slowly, over the printed mass,

Not wanting to disturb it as it basked in the sunshine,
Tiptoeing in to net it. I reached CUNCTATION,
Which means delay, delaying, or tardy action;
    Turned the page, to CUNNING, under the reading
                                                    glass.

I was sure I should see it, what a triumph! Quietly
I moved on to CUNSTER, a conner once in
                                        Scotland . . .
And then, in upper and lower case, I saw it:
    Cunt –: see CONT. Injustice! Under-represented!

When COCK is there in glory with words like
                                    CLAPPERDUDGEON
(Meaning a man who was born and bred a beggar).
So I turned to CONT, in a mood of disappointment.
    It's 'To punt (a boat, or barge)' over inland
                                            waterways!

PUNT for CUNT! That dictionary was joking!
Surely some scholar was laughing his head off!
I passed on, to the Supplement (CHIP–SPARROW,
                                            CLEAVAGE).
    Still not there! What sadness, under the microscope

No wonderful butterfly opening wings and closing
Or even frozen timelessly in grave lexicography –
Absent without leave, as they said in my Army days!
    Shut the book and put it back, with the reading
                                                    glass.

The Song of the Old Soldier

Across the miles and miles of burning plain
the Army's marching, marching, and marching yet
again.
Oh, yes, the fucking Army
is the terror of the land
and where the sea is wavy
you can see the sodding Navy –
but miles and miles above us,
where they can't raise a stand,
is the airy fairy Air Force with its joystick in its hand!

Across the miles and miles of frozen kelp
the Army's marching, marching, and marching
without help.
Oh, yes, the fucking Army
is the terror of the girls –
there are fewer girls than gravy
for the poor old sodding Navy,
and miles and miles above us,
like the swine above the pearls,
is the airy fairy Air Force with its profile and its curls!

Across the miles and miles of mountain range
the Army's marching, marching, and marching
without change.
The fearless fucking Army
leaves the babies in its wake,
while young Dan is doing Davy
in the silly sodding Navy –
but miles and miles above us,
drifting on without a brake,
is the airy fairy Air Force like a fancy piece of cake!

Drinker to Lover, Drunkard to Lecher

A glass of wine
won't say *No!*
or *Don't!* or *Let me go!*
You won't be asked
by any jar:
Who do you think you are?
You'll never hear
from pints of bitter
the hard words of a baby-sitter . . .

No double gin
answers back –
it hasn't got the knack –
it can't look pert,
annoyed or coy –
You're not my kind of boy
is something it
will never answer –
or yet *You're not much of a dancer!*

A vodka's smooth,
can be neat,
and vermouths can be very sweet –
they don't avoid
encroaching lips
or smack your fingertips.
They know their place,
won't fail to meet you,
and know exactly how to treat you!

Mr Ewart

Mr Ewart won't answer letters,
Mr Ewart is old and tired,
he is fed up with his betters
and his worses aren't admired.

Mr Ewart would like to founder
like an ancient worn-out ship
where the fathoms all sleep sounder
than the flake-outs on a trip.

Mr Ewart would like to vanish
with a minimum of fuss
either womanish or mannish,
or be run down by a bus.

Mr Ewart won't speak to people,
he is deaf, his eyes aren't good,
his response is now so feeble
you know he hasn't understood.

Mr Ewart is antisocial
and is quite opposed to fun,
all he knows is that much woe shall
come upon us – one by one.

Mr Ewart is sick of living,
he'd like quietly to lie down,
return the gifts that God is giving –
and get to Hell out of this town!

The Joys of Surgery

(dedicated to Richard Selzer, author of *Mortal Lessons*)

There's the riot and the rut –
when you make that first clean cut!
As the scarifying scalpel
makes you higher than an Alp'll –
blood appears in pretty beads,
that thin line directly leads
to the laid-bare opal fat,
you feel randy as a rat
and you don't lose much momentum
when you see the gauze omentum!

What's more horny than a heart
heaving with the surgeon's art?
and the clicking of the clips
is a series of short trips,
you're turned on, lit up, elationed –
quite as knocked out as the patient!
The abdomen's Aladdin's Cave
makes you want to rant and rave,
intestines, serpents of Old Nile,
curve and coil – you have to smile –
and you give a tender shiver
at the dark joy of the liver,
while the pink peritoneum,
lovely as an Art Museum,
strikes you with desire and dumb
till you very nearly come . . .

God made this delightful chasm
for your own intense orgasm!

A Putney Art Dealer is Censured by a Local Inhabitant for Displaying Detailed Female Nudes

Many people don't like pubic hair.
They say, quite simply: *It shouldn't be there!*
It's far too brash and bushy and animal.
In Art, it's often absent, minimal
or covered discreetly with swirls of drapery –
like pig's blood dropped on spotless napery,
reminds of the nature of the beast,
and sits like a ghost at the frolicsome feast.

Victorians thought it was coarse and crude,
although their painters quite loved the nude –
with 'Roman Baths' and 'The Wives of Hannibal',
enough plump flesh to entice a cannibal –

when it was safely in antiquity
it didn't smell of moral obliquity.
Puritans still, with our prudish fears,
we haven't changed much in a hundred years!

'The Sun' Also Rises

Oh, isn't it exciting!
There's going to be a war!!!
We hope there's lots of fighting –
we missed the one before!

Already men are drowning!
We're brave, we have no fear,
as patriots we're downing
our fearless pints of beer!

Two Harriers, one cruiser?
Our lads will put it right,
while we stay in the boozer
and carry on the fight . . .

Though we have high expenses
we shoot our mouths off quick,
large gins and their defences
are sure to do the trick!

At Death we're shouting 'Gotcha!',
we're perfect shining knights –
no diplomatic botcher
has any bleeding rights . . .

How grand for circulation
and for the Tories too,
a floor show for the Nation,
and free for me and you!

How grand for Mrs Thatcher –
she's almost out of sight!
Now Foot can never catch her,
though running day and night!

It's lovely on the telly,
home strategists agree,
when the Fascist underbelly
gets hit in time for tea!

We're full of warlike features –
and every word is priced –
despising spineless creatures
like peaceful Jesus Christ!

We know there's news in 'traitors' . . .
and as the hot war nears
like stripshow fornicators
we roar it on with cheers . . .
we hope it lasts for years!

20 May 1982

An English Don Wants to Go

Do I want to go to
that big crooked country
where the girls say
You don't know shit –
but you're kinda cute!
Do I want to go?

Yes, I want to go to
that amazing oil-rich country,
where the kids play
with bum and tit
and they're gonna shoot –
yes, I want to go!

138

Where my clipt, affected
English utterance
goes with the big stiff
old upper lip –
and I'm kinda mute,
with my English utterance!

Where entry's effected
by high-class utterance,
high as a cliff,
with a horsey clip –
and the campus will salute
my most English utterance!

The Retirement from Rugby Football of Bill Beaumont

Oh, what a wonderful winsome match-winning
                                    walrus
        has left our part of the sea!
Even in Scotland (where they thrive on broken play)
        and in Wales (where they fancy themselves)
        all the Rugger fans agree!

Captain of England in twenty-one mind-bending
                                    matches,
        and that includes a Grand Slam!
Leader of Lions (what a pride!) where tourists roar,
        he quite steadily pushed on ahead –
        without razzamatazz, POW or WHAM!

He started at Fylde, but before that (and clumsy) at
                                    Ellesmere
        at school he was a full-back.
He led by example (he *grew* into the captaincy,
        say the journalists); humour, hard work,
        they were his form of attack!

139

He never put the boot in or (nearly) squeezed
                                    somebody's balls off,
            his play was remarkably clean.
He had the ability to win the ball when
            it really mattered – what more could you
                                                want?
            He was magnificent, but not mean.

Andy Irvine, Ollie Campbell (those great ones) have
                                    both paid tribute
            to the best Captain they've known.
He wasn't commercial, he just loved Rugby,
            so solid, lumbering, rollerlike, steaming,
            wholesome, well-loved and home-grown!

But now a new computerized axial tomography scan
            has shown damage to the occiput.
From a fair kick on the head. And it's curtains
            (the Press says sadly) for ever and ever
            for his England boot and its foot!

Literary Bios

Was she a bitch? Was he a swine?
Oh, which was which? Both yours and mine,
before it's cut, the thread's a tangle.
It all depends on the different angle.

Was she an angel? and was he *good*?
Something strange'll be understood –
some behaved well, some behaved badly,
the happiest ones could end so sadly.

Louis MacNice? Louis MacNasty?
Pearl without price – or pretty ghastly?
He or she, the shot-silk colour
has a two-way shine that gets no duller.

Wystan, Dylan, doubtful smile,
Duke of Milan, or egophile –
the bountiful bios all come running
to say how stupid! how simply stunning!

The Owl Writes a Detective Story

A stately home where doves, in dovecotes, coo –
fields where calm cattle stand and gently moo,
trim lawns where croquet is the thing to do.
This is the ship, the house party's the crew:
Lord Feudal, hunter of the lion and gnu,
whose walls display the heads of not a few,
Her Ladyship, once Ida Fortescue,
who, like his Lordship very highborn too
surveys the world with a disdainful moue.
Their son – most active with a billiard cue –
Lord Lazy (stays in bed till half past two).
A Balkan Count called Popolesceru
(an ex-Dictator waiting for a coup).
Ann Fenn, most English, modest, straight and true,
a very pretty girl without a sou.
Adrian Finkelstein, a clever Jew.
Tempest Bellairs, a beauty such as you
would only find in books like this (she'd sue
if I displayed her to the public view –
enough to say men stick to her like glue).
John Huntingdon, who's only there to woo
(a fact, except for her, the whole house knew)
Ann Fenn. And, last, the witty Cambridge Blue,
the Honourable Algy Playfair, who
shines in detection. His clear 'View halloo!'
puts murderers into a frightful stew.

But now the plot unfolds! What *déjà vu*!
There! In the snow! – The clear print of a shoe!
Tempest is late for her next rendez-vous,
Lord Feudal's blood spreads wide – red, sticky goo

on stiff white shirtfront – Lazy's billet-doux
has missed Ann Fenn, and Popolesceru
has left – without a whisper of adieu
or saying goodbye, typical *mauvais gout*!
Adrian Finkelstein, give him his due,
behaves quite well. Excitement is taboo
in this emotionless landowner's zoo.
Algy, with calm that one could misconstrue
(handling with nonchalance bits of vertu)
knows who the murderer is. He has a clue.

But who? But who? Who, who, who, who, who, who?

NOTE   *This poem was written to be read aloud, and the
'oo' sounds at the ends of the lines should be intoned like the
call of an owl.*